THE NEW MERMAIDS

A Trick to Catch the Old One

THE NEW MERMAIDS

General Editors

PHILIP BROCKBANK
Professor of English, York University

BRIAN MORRIS
Senior Lecturer in English, York University

A Trick to Catch the Old One

THOMAS MIDDLETON

Edited by G. J. WATSON

ERNEST BENN LIMITED
LONDON

First published in this form 1968
by Ernest Benn Limited
Bouverie House · Fleet Street · London · EC4

© *Ernest Benn Limited 1968*

Distributed in Canada by
The General Publishing Company Limited · Toronto

Printed in Great Britain

510 – 34146 – 2

P/B 510 – 34151 – 9

TO
MY PARENTS

CONTENTS

ACKNOWLEDGEMENTS

DYCE's edition of Middleton's *Works* (1840) provided the basis for Bullen's standard edition of 1885, and all editors of Middleton are in their debt. I have also made use of Havelock Ellis's original *Mermaid* edition of *A Trick* (1887). Other modern editions, particularly those of Sampson (in *Thomas Middleton*, New York, 1915), of Spencer (in *Elizabethan Plays*, Boston, 1933), and of Baskervill, Heltzel and Nethercot (in *Elizabethan and Stuart Plays*, New York, 1934), have provided some useful suggestions.

A number of articles on Middleton's early comedies, such as those of Samuel Schoenbaum and R. B. Parker, have proved valuable.

I am also grateful to Dr Brian Morris for his helpful advice and criticism.

ABBREVIATIONS

1. Texts of *A Trick*:

Q1 = The first edition, 1608.
Q2 = The second edition, 1616.
Dyce = A. Dyce, ed., *The Works of Thomas Middleton*, 5 vols., ii, 1840.
Bullen = A. H. Bullen, ed., *The Works of Thomas Middleton*, 8 vols., ii, 1885.
Ellis = H. Ellis, ed., *Thomas Middleton*, The Mermaid Series, 2 vols., i, 1887.
Sampson = M. W. Sampson, ed., *Thomas Middleton*, New York, 1915.
Spencer = H. Spencer, ed., *Elizabethan Plays*, Boston, 1933.
Baskervill = C. R. Baskervill *et al.*, edd., *Elizabethan and Stuart Plays*, New York, 1934.

2. Other works:

Bowers = F. Bowers, ed., *The Dramatic Works of Thomas Dekker*, 4 vols., 1953–61.
Chambers = E. K. Chambers, *The Elizabethan Stage*, 4 vols., 1923.
Greg = W. W. Greg, *A Bibliography of the English Printed Drama to the Restoration*, 4 vols., 1939–59.
Grosart = A. B. Grosart, ed., *The Life and Complete Works in Prose and Verse of Robert Greene*, 15 vols., 1881–6.
Herford and Simpson = C. H. Herford and P. and E. Simpson, edd., *Ben Jonson*, 11 vols., 1925–52.
OED = *The Oxford English Dictionary*.
Tilley = M. P. Tilley, *A Dictionary of Proverbs in England in the Sixteenth and Seventeenth Centuries*, Ann Arbor, 1950.
Quotations from and references to Shakespeare are from the Oxford edition of W. J. Craig, 1905.

3. Journals:

EC = *Essays in Criticism*
HLQ = *Huntington Library Quarterly*
JEGP = *Journal of English and Germanic Philology*
Library = *The Library, a quarterly review of Bibliography*
MLN = *Modern Language Notes*
MLR = *Modern Language Review*
NQ = *Notes and Queries*

PMLA = *Publications of the Modern Language Association of America*
RES = *Review of English Studies*
RN = *Renaissance News*
SB = *Studies in Bibliography*
SP = *Studies in Philology*

INTRODUCTION

THE AUTHOR

THOMAS MIDDLETON was born in London in 1580. His father, a man of some substance, a 'citizen and brick-layer', died when Thomas was only five years old and his school and university studies were clearly pursued against a turbulent, litigious background of suits raised by his mother against his adventurer stepfather. Although he matriculated at Queen's College, Oxford, in 1598, he probably did not take a degree.

In 1597 he published his first work, *The Wisdom of Solomon Paraphrased* (described by Swinburne as 'a tideless and interminable sea of fruitless and inexhaustible drivel') followed by other pamphlets in prose and verse. By 1600 he was settled in London 'daylie accompaninge the players', and by 1603 Middleton, now married, was writing comedies for Henslowe and others.

Throughout the first ten or fifteen years of the century Middleton wrote many successful comedies and intrigues of town life. In such plays as *Michaelmas Term, A Mad World, My Masters* and *A Trick to Catch the Old One*, Middleton casts a sardonic eye on the seamy side of London life. But his satire differs greatly in tone and technique from that of Jonson and Marston, who also wrote sophisticatedly satiric plays for the private theatres. Middleton eschews their explicit castigation of vice—his own moral judgement is implicit and ironically understated. Likewise his much-discussed 'realism' is in interesting contrast to the exaggeration and distortion typical of Jonsonian satire. Jonson's distortions insist on the abnormality of vice, whereas Middleton's disarmingly 'realistic' and dead-pan presentation of a completely venal world enables him to insinuate that vice is normal. This is perfectly sound satiric strategy, but many critics have missed the irony and have condemned Middleton's comedies as immoral.

Around twenty-five plays have been definitely attributed to Middleton. Collaboration with Webster, Dekker, Beaumont and Rowley helped to give variety to his output: e.g. *A Fair Quarrel*, in collaboration with Rowley, is a tragi-comedy of a very different outlook from his other plays, with its discussion of 'honour' and the ethics of duelling. There is, in fact, considerable variety in Middleton's output: comedies, tragi-comedies, pageants and masques for city occasions (he became City Chronologer in 1620), a political satire, *A Game at Chess*, which caused a furore and may have led to the author's imprisonment, and two great tragedies, *Women Beware Women* and *The Changeling*. He died in 1627.

THE DATE

No internal evidence exists to help in establishing a date of composition, though most authorities[1] concur in placing it between 1604 and 1606, and agree that 1606 is likeliest. A terminal limit is set by the fact that the play belonged to the Paul's boys. The company cannot be traced after 30 July 1606 when they performed a play now lost before King James and the king of Denmark,[2] and there is evidence that their playing was discontinued soon after. *A Trick* was entered by George Eld on the Stationers' Register on 7 October 1607 and printed soon after.[3]

Structurally the play is extremely assured and seems to have been written late in the series of early comedies. It has a classically shaped plot, based on a single well-contrived stratagem, unlike *Michaelmas Term*, *Your Five Gallants* and even *A Mad World, My Masters*, where all the emphasis falls on the multiplicity and intricacy of the intriguers' schemes, often (as in *Your Five Gallants*, the most episodic of the early plays) to the detriment of overall dramatic unity.

It is difficult to substantiate this impression that *A Trick* comes late in the sequence of Middleton's early comedies. No internal or external evidence exists which might establish the date of the play, and what follows is necessarily hypothetical. There are certain similarities between *A Trick* and Ben Jonson's *Volpone*, first played

---

[1] Chambers, *Eliz. Stage*, iii, 439; R. C. Bald, 'The Chronology of Middleton's Plays', *MLR*, XXXII (1937), 37; R. H. Barker, *Thomas Middleton*, New York, 1958, p. 165; A. Harbage, *Annals of English Drama, 975–1700*, revised S. Schoenbaum, 1964, p. 90.

[2] See Chambers, *op. cit.*, ii, 22.

[3] The title pages of the two issues, both dated 1608, of the first edition of *A Trick*, establish that the Children of Blackfriars took the play over from the disbanded Paul's boys, performing it before the king on 1 January 1609, since it is only during 1608/9 that they are recorded as appearing at court. Greg notes that the date on the second imprint may be taken as indicating the legal and not the calendar year, though 'it . . . may have been retained inadvertently' (*Bibl. Drama*, i, item 262). But G. R. Price, in a very recent article in *The Library*, argues persuasively that there was an unrecorded court performance on New Year's night 1607 and that the play was printed in December of that year.

about the middle of March 1606,[4] which suggest a 1606 date for the former. The subject-matter of the plays, the legacy hunting of the one and the rich widow hunting of the other, have much in common, and many features of dramatic technique correspond as a result of the basic similarity of theme. In each play a single stratagem articulates the intrigue[5]—all the shifts of the action are due to a clever schemer's manipulation of the other characters' greed for his own financial gain. More specifically, the three creditors of *A Trick* resemble the three birds of prey in *Volpone* in their unctuous flattery of their deceiver, in their competitive suspiciousness about one another, and in the uncharacteristic liberality to which they drive themselves in hope of fat rewards. Their malevolence when they discover they have been duped is also similar. Middleton groups his sharks round the bait of the supposed rich widow to give a typically Jonsonian perspective of avaricious folly: the host, the creditors, Moneylove, Hoard and Lucre all evince the same mercenary relish when they hear of her. Just as Corbaccio disinherits his son in hope of Volpone's fortune, so Lucre disinherits his grandson in the hope that 'some of the widow's lands, too, may one day fall upon me if things be carried wisely' (II. i, 171-2). As Mosca allows each of the prospective legatees of Volpone to see the gifts that have been brought by others, so Witgood similarly arouses the competitive and avaricious spirit in his uncle (see III. i, 251-8). Nevertheless, these resemblances are not at all conclusive.

Corroborative evidence, however, for dating *A Trick* some time after late 1605 or early 1606 is provided by Dekker and Webster's *Northward Ho!*, acted at the end of 1605,[6] the sub-plot of which concerns the doings of Doll Hornet, a London whore who decides to repair her fortunes by 'giving it out' that she is a rich gentlewoman. The play has, in common with *A Trick*, the deception of suitors in order to gain money from them, a young man who deceives an older relative about the true identity of the whore, the whore's marriage to somebody more interested in her money than herself, and the final revelation of the true state of affairs. The hypothesis that Middleton knew *Northward Ho!* and may have been influenced by it is strengthened by a number of verbal parallels between the two plays (see especially V. ii, 158-66 and notes); and it may be significant that *Northward Ho!*, like *A Trick*, was acted by the Children of Paul's, and that during 1604 Middleton had collaborated with Dekker in the first part of *The Honest Whore*.

[4] See Herford and Simpson, ii, 49, n. 1.

[5] In his other city comedies, Middleton interweaves two, or even, as in *A Chaste Maid in Cheapside*, 1611, four stories in the same plot.

[6] Chambers, *Eliz. Stage*, iii, 295.

It is true that the resemblances between *A Trick* and *Northward Ho!* and *Volpone* are very general, and I do not suggest that these plays were the only or even the major inspiration for Middleton's play. But until more conclusive evidence turns up, a date in the first half of 1606 fits all the known facts about the presentation of the play, and accords with the vaguer and less satisfactory evidence of style and influence.[7]

THE SOURCES

It has been argued that the plot of *A Trick* may have been suggested by that of the *Persa* of Plautus.[8] In this, the clever slave Toxilus schemes to raise money to buy his love from the pimp Dordalus. With the help of a fellow slave, Toxilus persuades Dordalus to buy the daughter of the parasite Saturio whom he passes off as a kidnapped rich Persian girl. Dordalus, deluded by reports of her wealth, by her aristocratic behaviour, and even more by reflection on how much money he can make from her, buys her for a considerable price. With this sum Toxilus buys his own love's freedom; subsequently, Dordalus discovers to his horror that his Persian is really a Roman citizen (and, *ipso facto*, free), and is jeered at and flouted by the celebrating slaves.

Although there is some similarity, however, it is unlikely that Middleton used the *Persa* as the source for *A Trick*. The plots of the classical 'New Comedy' are highly conventional, and many analogues to the plot of the *Persa*, built on impersonation and the duping of tight-fisted fathers and pimps, can be found not only in other plays by Plautus but in the 'erudite' or more formal Renaissance comedy of both Italy and England, which the Roman drama influenced greatly.[9] Further, the handling of each plot is quite different: the transference of interest from the ingenuity and vitality of the

---

[7] A. J. Sabol, 'Ravenscroft's "Melismata" and the Children of Paul's', *RN*, XII (1959), 3–9, who discovered that the song which opens IV.v is by Ravenscroft, argues that since he took his Cambridge degree in 1605, the play must have been written before then. I do not see that this is necessarily so, since Ravenscroft maintained his associations with the stage for many years (see W. J. Lawrence, 'Thomas Ravenscroft's Theatrical Associations', *MLR*, XIX (1924), 418–23).

[8] S. Falk, 'Plautus' *Persa* and Middleton's *A Trick to Catch the Old One*', *MLN*, LXVI (1951), 19–21.

[9] G. E. Duckworth, *The Nature of Roman Comedy*, Princeton, 1952, pp. 396–424, and Madeleine Doran, *Endeavours of Art*, Madison, 1954, pp. 148–82, give useful general accounts of this influence.

deceivers in the Roman play to the greed and folly of the deceived in Middleton's, and the extension of the motivation of avarice to almost all of his characters, renders *A Trick* much more like Jonsonian satiric comedy than Plautine farcical intrigue. It is useful to be reminded, however, in the light of the prevailing critical insistence on Middleton's documentary 'realism', that the play belongs to an old stage tradition.

It is just possible that Middleton may owe the device whereby the usurer marries the rich widow by fraud only to discover she is nothing but a witty adventuress to an English jest-book, *The Twelve Merry Jests of the Widow Edith*,[10] which describes how the 'widow' arouses and makes gain of the cupidity of men by representing herself as rich. When they become suitors and in the expectation of plenty have heaped sufficient gifts on her, she decamps with her plunder to try her ruse elsewhere. There is no positive means of demonstrating that Middleton knew the jest-book; but it seems possible, given his considerable interest in rogue literature (Robert Greene's coney-catching pamphlets were the most important single non-dramatic influence on Middleton's other early comedies, and something of Greene's world and vocabulary can be perceived in *A Trick*); and the fact that an episode in a later play, *Anything for a Quiet Life* (1621), resembles in most respects the sixth merry jest, is also suggestive.[11] But Edith has many relatives in folk literature; and the resemblances between her and Middleton's courtesan are merely broadly generic, like those between the latter and the roistering, bawdy Doll Hornet of *Northward Ho!*

It is, in fact, misguided to look for any single source for *A Trick*. Middleton's materials are the stock-in-trade of the comic stage. Witgood, for instance, is a synthesis of many conventional character-types. He is first of all a Jacobean version of the prodigal son, a 'rioter', a 'wastethrift', a 'penurious makeshift', a 'brotheller', a 'surfeiter', a 'riotous undone man', a 'spendthrift dissolute fellow', and all these appellations place him firmly in the prodigal play tradition. This in itself was a composite dramatic form, deriving from the treatment in Terentian comedy of the problems of the education of the *adulescens*, and from the English moralities dealing with the temptation of youth, as well as from the Dutch education drama of the sixteenth century which combined the story of the Prodigal

---

[10] Editions in 1525 and 1573, reprinted in W. C. Hazlitt's *Shakespeare Jest-Books*, 1864, iii, 27–108, and discussed by A. W. Reed, *Early Tudor Drama*, 1926, pp. 156–9.
[11] See M. G. Christian, *Non-Dramatic Sources for the Rogues in Middleton's Plays*, Chicago, 1936.

with the forms and spirit of Latin comedy.[12] Secondly, Witgood is to a certain extent the gallant, an established literary type appearing not only in contemporary drama but in the formal satire of the 1590's and the Character writers. He is also related to the well-spoken rogue of many of Greene's coney-catching pamphlets, and of a work like *The Merry Conceited Jests of George Peele*.[13]

Hoard and Lucre belong to an even more popular literary brotherhood, that of the usurer, and, though they are vigorously presented, it is again important to realise how heavily Middleton is drawing on a stock literary type. What is more, the events of the plot, and the relationship which ties Witgood to Hoard and Lucre, are part of an honourable English stage tradition (though again much is owed to 'New Comedy'). A. B. Stonex has traced in about sixty comedies of the Elizabethan and Jacobean period the evolution and flowering of what he calls 'the prodigal-usurer play':

> The typical and excellent comic situation . . . is this: a young spend-thrift, who has become heavily indebted, or has actually lost his property to a usurer, comes into his own, or the other's, property by eloping with the usurer's daughter and by carrying off anything else of value . . . A somewhat similar, though really distinct and later device for undoing the usurer . . . was the introduction of an heiress whose hand both should seek, but of course the prodigal should eventually win.[14]

A Trick is obviously a refined specimen of this genre, but it is nevertheless of it—as Stonex goes on to say

> There is practically no end to the dexterous changes that were wrought in these two basic groupings of character and events.

A Trick, then, is shaped by well-established traditions of the comic stage, and we should think of parallels rather than of sources for it. The main point is the thorough-going literary conventionality of the material, which must be stressed since Middleton is so often praised as a kind of detailed transcriber of the contemporary scene. It is rather in the selection and arrangement of his conventional material that he shows himself an interesting and original dramatist.

[12] For discussions of the tradition, and lists of its examplars in English drama, see R. W. Bond, *Early Plays from the Italian*, 1911, pp. xciii–cviii, and F. Schelling, *Elizabethan Drama*, Boston and New York, 1908, i, 63–7.
[13] See M. G. Christian, *op. cit.*
[14] 'The Usurer in Elizabethan Drama', *PMLA*, XXXI (1916), 196–7. Some of the better-known plays to a greater or lesser degree within this type are *The Jew of Malta*, 1589, *The Merchant of Venice*, 1596, *Eastward Ho!*, 1605, and Massinger's *A New Way to Pay Old Debts*, 1621, which is indebted to *A Trick* for its central situation.

THE PLAY

The subject-matter of *A Trick* is avarice, the power of money, and the gullibility of men who pursue it, and Middleton gives depth to his theme by showing a whole society motivated by greed. Thus, although Witgood has youth, intelligence and the conventional romantic interest—very scantily treated—on his side, he is a thoroughly mercenary operator. His opening speech concerns his status as a gentleman, the necessity of raising some money to preserve that status, and (eventually) his ambition to marry Hoard's niece, an aim in which her 'portion' seems to weigh as much as her 'virtues'. [15] He is extremely purposive even if to a certain extent driven by the laws of necessity. He himself sees his 'wit' as a product of this necessity, not (like Chapman's young intriguers, and even Volpone) as a form of self-expression and self-delight. Thus, his wit is his 'last means' (I. i, 29), a necessary tool in the battle for survival in an acquisitive society:

> I perceive there's nothing conjures up wit sooner than poverty, and nothing lays it down sooner than wealth and lechery (III. i, 83–5).

He does not direct all the action: the Hoard-courtesan complication is not engineered by him, and the final gulling of Hoard by the pre-contract trick is the result of some brilliant—and desperate—improvisation. It is not a witty flourish. In fact, the courtesan rebukes Witgood for it, and he defends his stratagem on the grounds of necessity (IV. iv, 170–4). The priority is, in short, money, and Witgood exults more in the recovery of his mortgage, serenaded at IV. ii, 87–92 in terms which would be more appropriate for Joyce, than in his marriage, to which he gives a perfunctory nod in the final scene. Mercenariness dictates his personal relationships: his first words to the likeable courtesan are a rebuke to her for having been 'the consumption of my purse', and he later advises her to marry Hoard because

> He's rich in money, moveables, and lands; marry him, he's an old doting fool, and that's worth all. (III. i, 110–12)

But Witgood is only one predatory man among many. A comparison with the *Persa* may help to illustrate the basically satiric organisation of Middleton's plot. In the *Persa*, the interest centres on the actual management and progress of the intrigue, and no moral point emerges—or need be made—from the spectacle of the outwitting of a conventionally nasty stage type by his witty antagonists.

[15] Joyce's wealth is mentioned again at I. i, 134 and II. i, 337.

On the other hand, Witgood need only launch the 'rich widow' into his society and exploit the situations which the resultant rush of sharks to the bait causes. His role is much less active than that of Toxilus—he does not appear at the crucial points where Lucre and Hoard fall victims to their own greed. The only deception, in fact, in which Witgood plays an active part is his duping of the host, whom he needs as an accomplice. Even in this scene (I. ii), and increasingly throughout the remainder of the action, cupidity plays a bigger part in the deceptions than the skill of the deceiver: Witgood can retire from the centre of the scene to watch the forces he has set in motion work themselves out. Lucre is hooked first by the hope that 'some of the widow's lands, too, may one day fall upon me if things be carried wisely' (II. i, 171–2); Mrs Lucre wants the widow for her son Sam; Moneylove seeks Hoard's aid so that he can 'set fair' for four hundred a year; the creditors nose out the rumour of wealth and rush to press money on Witgood; finally Hoard himself turns his considerable energies to the hunt, not merely to repay Lucre for formerly out-swindling him, but also

> to enrich my state, augment my revenues, and build mine own
> fortunes greater. (II. ii, 44–5)

What Witgood began as a stratagem to get some money from his uncle snowballs into a series of situations in which the cupidity of those around him, rather than his own endeavours, solves all his problems.

However, Witgood himself does not escape Middleton's ironic glance. One of the neatest moments in a play distinguished by neat ironies occurs when the creditors, now knowing that Hoard has got the widow, are trying to recover their money from Witgood. He feigns reluctance to sign a release in return for Hoard's paying off his debts, and they take him aside:

1 CREDITOR
> Take hold of his offer; pax on her, let her go. If your debts were once discharged, I would help you to a widow myself worth ten of her.

3 CREDITOR
> Mass, partner, and now you remember me on't, there's Master Mulligrub's sister newly fallen a widow.

1 CREDITOR
> Cuds me, as pat as can be! There's a widow left for you, ten thousand in money, beside plate, jewels, *et cetera*.
>   (IV. iv, 197–203)

And Witgood takes the bait: at the first opportunity he gets, when alone with the creditors, he returns to the subject:

> A word sir; what, will you carry me to that rich widow now?

only to be told ' 'Twas a trick we have amongst us to get in our money' (IV. iv, 270–5). The appearance of the rich fiancée on a balcony at this point and Witgood's fervent 'My life!' brilliantly emphasise the irony of the biter-bit situation. Witgood's readiness for the hunt-the-widow game formally completes the circle of cupidity described by the plot.

This acquisitive set of sharks is placed in a wider perspective of venality. Thus, there are the widow-hunters whom one never sees, conjured up by Witgood:

> Here comes one old gentleman, and he'll make her a jointure of three hundred a year, forsooth; another wealthy suitor will estate his son in his lifetime, and make him weigh down the widow; here a merchant's son will possess her with no less than three goodly lordships at once, which were all pawns to his father;
>
> (III. i, 253–8)

and their counterparts, the hunters of the rich heir, pictured by Lucre:

> jolly rich widows have been offered him here i'th' city, great merchants' wives . . . if he were once known to be in town, he would be presently sought after; nay, and happy were they that could catch him first . . . there would be such running to and fro, widow, he should not pass the streets for 'em.   (II. i, 310–19)

Witgood remarks that 'there's nothing like the bringing of a widow to one's uncle's house' (II. i, 231–2), and Lucre, having done all in his power to deceive the 'widow' about the reality of Witgood's wealth, complacently accepts the compliment to his genius for exploitation—

> many a match has been struck up in my house a' this fashion: let 'em try all manner of ways, still there's nothing like an uncle's house to strike the stroke in.   (II. i, 333–5)

Dampit boasts of having made his clients 'follow me with their purses . . . and I soused 'em with bills of charges' (I. iv, 63–6). All this serves to heighten our impression of a thoroughly rapacious society, and we see from Witgood's cynical congratulation to the courtesan, when Hoard has been ensnared, that rapacity takes more than one form:

> Give you joy, Mistress Hoard; I promise your fortune was good, forsooth; y'ave fell upon wealth enough, and there's young gentlemen enow can help you to the rest.   (III. i, 238–41)

Besides enlarging the context of his plot in this way Middleton keeps us constantly aware that the predatory mentality governs his dramatic world. Many details emphasise this concept of exploitation—for

instance, Lucre's casual reference to his 'last purchase' (i.e., swindle,
II. i, 198), or a figure of speech like the host's rhetorical

> Come forfeitures to a usurer, fees to an officer, punks to an host
> . . . desiredly?   (I. ii, 17–18)

Middleton, then, presents a society which is, in its own way, just as
mercenary as that of *Volpone*. But his satiric methods, which give
the play its distinctively personal tone, differ widely from Jonson's.
The early 'comical satires' of both Jonson and Marston are completely controlled by the desire to hold folly up to overt ridicule, and
their most significant character is the malcontent satirist, or railer, of
varying degrees of acerbity and moral rectitude, violently lashing
vice and often manipulating the action to bring about the exposure
and discomfiting of folly.[16] Although in *Volpone* Jonson considerably
modifies his early satirical technique (particularly in discarding the
satiric commentator, or moralist, within the play), the didactic note is
as pronounced, the ethical position as clear, and the moral judgement
as uncompromisingly firm as ever. Volpone and Mosca, for instance,
take over in part the function of the critical commentator in con-
sistently directing our attention to the vices of their dupes,[17] and they
and the dupes are unequivocally condemned and harshly punished
at the end of the play. Even without these explicit moral sign-posts,
however, we would not be in danger of losing our ethical bearings.
In the hyperbole of Volpone's invocations to his gold and to Celia,
in the pervasive imagery of the beast-fable, in the presence of the
dwarf, eunuch and hermaphrodite, who symbolise the moral ugliness
of their putative father, Jonson exaggerates and distorts, to thrust on
us a sense of the abnormality of vice. Finally Jonson, like Marston,
found that a foreign setting, and in particular the sophisticated and
notoriously wicked Venice, suited his essentially exaggerative satiric
technique.

In *A Trick*, however, Middleton suppresses as far as possible
the accent of moral condemnation. What lends his best comedies
their individual flavour is the dispassionate presentation of vice.
Middleton suggests that vice is normal, that it is the natural way of
the world. This simple, but extremely effective, satiric concept

[16] For full accounts of the comical satires of Jonson and Marston, see O. J.
Campbell, *Comicall Satyre and Shakespeare's 'Troilus and Cressida'*, San
Marino, 1938, and A. B. Kernan, *The Cankered Muse*, New Haven, 1959.
One of Middleton's earlier plays, *The Phoenix*, 1604, is an unsatisfactory
experiment in the Jonson–Marston style.
[17] See R. Nash, 'The Comic Intent of *Volpone*', *SP*, XLIV (1947), 26–40.
He points out that Jonson's masterpieces 'develop and improve, rather than
abandon, the methods of his "comical satyres" '.

helps to explain the most distinctive features of his art: the pervasive irony, which replaces explicit castigation of vice, and the much-praised realism, which replaces Jonsonian exaggeration and distortion, and is a necessary technical support of the ironic suggestion that vice is normal. *A Trick* shows the method at its characteristic best.

As a survey of the action and its social context shows, Middleton excludes good characters from his world: there are no righteously indignant spokesmen for morality nor any hint that there are scales of value other than driving mercenariness in the society in which the action is set. The characters themselves accept the vicious sharking as entirely natural, just the way of the world, as the courtesan remarks. For example, Onesiphorus explains that the Hoard-Lucre animosity is due to a quarrel about

> a purchase, fetching over a young heir; Master Hoard, my brother, having wasted much time in beating the bargain, what did me old Lucre, but as his conscience moved him, knowing the poor gentleman, stepped in between 'em and cozened him himself
>
> (I. i, 114–18)

and Limber asks in surprise 'And was this all, sir?' Hoard and Lucre have a violent argument about this swindle, and Lucre gives perfect expression to the mentality which dominates the world presented by Middleton:

> I got the purchase, true; was't not any man's case? Yes. Will a wise man stand as a bawd, whilst another wipes his nose of the bargain? No, I answer no in that case. (I. iii, 11–14)

In fact, the whole argument illustrates Middleton's ironic method very well, since it is concerned with etiquette—the question of priority in the swindling of the unfortunate heir—not with the morality of cheating itself, which is accepted casually, as a *donnée*—'was't not any man's case?'

Further, Lucre knew the poor gentleman, and *therefore* (it is implied) cheated him. Normal relationships are turned topsy-turvy in this society, and it is suggested that there is something particularly appropriate and natural in Lucre's swindling of his nephew. As Witgood says of the prodigal and his relations

> Let him that is his nearest kin
> Cheat him before a stranger.
> And that's his uncle, 'tis a principle in usury. (I. i, 16–18)

And Lucre laughs to himself about his friend—'I confess I had an uncle's pen'worth: let me see, half in half, true' (II. i, 7–8).

'Cousinship' and 'cozenage' are identified,[18] as Witgood celebrates the
return of his mortgage:

> We'll ne'er trust conscience of our kin
> Since cozenage brings that title in.   (IV. ii, 91–2)

Witgood's attitude to his victims is very different from that of
Volpone or Mosca. He is not interested in laughing at their folly,
and his chief dupe, Hoard, is entirely self-duped, Witgood having
no designs on him when the play opens. He sees the folly of Lucre
and Hoard less as enjoyably ridiculous than simply as potentially
profitable. He is too busy pursuing his own ends to pass moral
judgements: as he says himself, on the recovery of the mortgage,

> I do conceive such joy in mine own happiness,
> I have no leisure yet to laugh at their follies.   (IV. ii, 85–6)

The revelation of the courtesan's true identity at the end is accidental
—it is not planned to bring Hoard to a realisation of his ridiculous
mistake (compare Volpone's delight in organising and seeing the
disabusing of his dupes by Mosca in the will scene). The ending of
the play in other ways provides a significant contrast with the judgement scene in *Volpone*. Hoard and Lucre have been out-manoeuvred
and they, and their antagonist, see their defeat solely in these terms—
'the moral aspect of the situation is avoided', as R. B. Parker notes in
his perceptive essay.[19] The predatory creditors are paid and go unpunished, and Witgood and the courtesan despite the dubiousness
of their moral position escape any kind of retribution. The note of
reform sounded in their closing speeches is ironically undermined
by the detailed knowledge of marital infidelities and rake's practices
revealed in them. Indeed, the jingling, rhyming style of the two
passages suggests a burlesque of the traditionally moral exit of the
prodigal.

Middleton's 'realism' also has an important function in this
attempt to subdue the note of moral seriousness and to disguise the
ethical bent of the play. Thus, the scene in which the fantastic plot
is placed is thoroughly familiar: we hear of the 'motions' of Fleet
Street and Holborn, of Lucre's house at Highgate, of Barnard's Inn,
and are taken into a London tavern and to Cole Harbour. These and
similar details are not dwelt upon—Middleton is not concerned with

---

[18] The derivation of *cozen* is uncertain, but in the light of the ironic connection which Middleton makes between the concepts of cozenage and
kindred, the *OED*'s note on the word is interesting: 'It has generally been
associated with *cousin*, sb., and compared with F. *cousiner*, explained by
Cotgrave, 1611, as "to clayme kindred for aduantage, or particular ends".'
[19] 'Middleton's Experiments with Comedy and Judgement', *Stratford-upon-
Avon Studies*, edd. Brown and Harris, I (1960), 179–99.

giving the kind of topographical picture of London life which one finds in Haughton's *Englishmen for My Money* (1598) or in some of the work of Heywood and Dekker. The city for him is, rather, a natural home for the predatory greed which is his true subject; but this kind of easy, unforced reference to London districts and to normal aspects of the city's life found in *A Trick*, helps to give Middleton's society a 'deceptive solidity', and to hide the fact that it is extremely narrow and highly selective.[20]

Further, there is a 'realistic' presentation of character—Middleton eschews the distortion and exaggeration of Jonson's and Marston's satire. In the case of Hoard and Lucre, for instance, Middleton deliberately suppressed the conventional traits[21] which make the typical stage-usurer at once ridiculous and monstrous. Thus, their age is not stressed: in fact, there is a sense of buoyancy and vitality in Hoard's address to his livery men:

I am not so old but I have pleasant days to come. I promise you, my masters, I take such a good liking to you, that I entertain you all; I put you already into my countenance, and you shall be shortly in my livery . . . we shall have all our sports within ourselves; all the gentlemen o'th' country shall be beholding to us and our pastimes.
(IV. iv, 46–55)

The usurer in love is a traditionally ridiculous spectacle, but Hoard is no *vecchio innamorato*: the springs of his devotion to his young wife arise from his hard-headed appreciation of her 'manors, manor houses, parks, groves . . . together with all her cattle, money, plate, jewels' (IV. iv, 243–6). Neither character has the cough, the great nose, the spectacles and the gout of a conventional usurer. The traditional half-starved miser does not have groups of gentlemen friends, nor does he invite his servants to 'wash their lungs' in his buttery, nor his acquaintances to taste of his wine with the easy largesse of Hoard.

They are nevertheless usurers whose only real passion is competitive acquisitiveness;[22] Middleton, however, is concerned not

[20] M. C. Bradbrook, *The Growth and Structure of Elizabethan Comedy*, 1955, p. 159, discusses the superficiality of Middleton's social documentation. D. B. Dodson, 'Thomas Middleton's City Comedies', unpublished Ph.D. dissertation, Columbia University, 1954, p. 171, points to the significance of the London background in relation to the satirical method of the play: 'no attempt is made to develop the exotic appeal of Spanish, Italian, or French social deviation.' Marston and Jonson, on the other hand, tend to favour a superlatively wicked foreign setting.
[21] See C. T. Wright, 'Some Conventions Regarding the Usurer in Elizabethan Literature', *SP*, XXXI (1934), 176–97.
[22] '. . . cupidity is the sole power [in the play] . . . the mutual hatred of the two old men . . . which is the most passionate feature of the play, depends on their common devotion to wealth' (M. C. Bradbrook, *op. cit.*, p. 156).

with emphasising their monstrosity, but with trying to convince us that they are perfectly ordinary London businessmen. So Hoard greets his friends, 'Your fathers and mine were all free o'th' fishmongers' (V. ii, 21–2), and Lucre jocularly addresses his wife:

> ... thou'rt a fine cook, I know't; thy first husband married thee out of an alderman's kitchen; go to, he raised thee for raising of paste. What! here's none but friends; most of our beginnings must be winked at.   (IV. ii, 73–6)

Many other references link them to normal thriving city life. We do not see them gloating over money-bags, but rather as substantial citizens with town houses, servants and acquaintance with the nobility (note the entrance of Lady Foxstone in V. ii). This impression of bourgeois respectability is strengthened by the tone of moral outrage which both Lucre and Hoard adopt in regard to Witgood's prodigality ('Why may not a virtuous uncle have a dissolute nephew? ... must sin in him call up shame in me?').

Middleton also presents their ambitions as 'realistic': he does not exaggerate their acquisitive drive to make the moral point. This is easily illustrated by comparing the limitless desires of Volpone and of Sir Epicure Mammon (in Jonson's *The Alchemist*), which are deliberately exaggerated to Marlovian heights, with Hoard's blissful imaginings:

> she's worth four hundred a year in her very smock ... But the journey will be all, in troth, into the country; to ride to her lands in state and order following my brother and other worshipful gentlemen, whose companies I ha' sent down for already, to ride along with us in their goodly decorum beards, their broad velvet cassocks, and chains of gold twice or thrice double; against which time I'll entertain some ten men of mine own into liveries, all of occupations or qualities: I will not keep an idle man about me. (IV. iv, 8–17)

This is firmly anchored to the realities of Jacobean life, the lyricism chained by the prose. For Lucre, too, 'four hundred a year in good rubbish' is the height of a concrete, realisable ambition.

The mode of the play is, then, 'realistic': the familiarity of the scene is stressed, and exaggeration and satirical distortion is greatly played down. It is important to see that this 'realism' is a satirical technique, extremely useful to Middleton's ironic suggestion that vice is normal. It is not an end in itself. The point needs to be stressed, as it has been traditional to see Middleton's work as that of a documentary realist. Schelling was one of the first to express this widely held account of 'the most absolute realist in the Elizabethan drama'; Archer describes *A Trick* as 'a spirited transcript of contemporary life'; and T. S. Eliot puts it even more strongly:

There is little doubt . . . that Middleton's comedy was 'photographic', that it introduces us to the low life of the time far better than anything in the comedy of Shakespeare or the comedy of Jonson, better than anything except the pamphlets of Dekker and Greene and Nashe.[23]

But, as a survey of the literary conventionality of Middleton's 'sources' for *A Trick* shows, this documentary, 'photographic' quality in his realism is open to question, and those who look for Jacobean social documentation, of other than the most general kind, in the play will be sadly disappointed. This is not to deny that his dramatic world had any basis in actuality;[24] but to think of Middleton as *primarily* a 'realist' leads to distorted interpretations of his plays, and in the case of *A Trick*, overlooks the highly formal quality of the art. Above all, it overlooks the fact that satire may have many aspects, the ironic and realistically deadpan, as well as the obviously didactic. In short, the 'realism' of Middleton's plays is important only in so far as it lends seeming authentication to the satiric assertion that fraudulence and cozenage are the social norms.

So the outrageous attitudes and situations of *A Trick* are presented without the slightest hint of moral agitation, as if they were perfectly natural. A measure of the success of Middleton's sophisticated and insidious technique is indicated by the very number of critics who see him as a photographic realist, and by another school of critics who are uneasy about the absence of conventional moral signposts. Symons complains that Middleton 'is no more careful of his ethical than of his other probabilities'; L. B. Wright objects to the absence of good characters from *A Trick*, and L. C. Knights has a similar point of view:

> The ambition of Hoard . . . is not set in the light of a positive ideal of citizen conduct (something that we find . . . in the work of Dekker and Heywood, dramatists inferior to Middleton).

Harbage objects to the end of the play, feeling it wrong that Witgood goes unpunished, and complaining that the courtesan 'orates in defence of harlotry'; C. M. Gayley felt likewise, and though he admits 'the literary and dramatic excellence' of *A Trick*, considers Middleton's comedies to be without exception 'cinematographs of

[23] Schelling, *Elizabethan Drama*, i, 516; W. Archer, *The Old Drama and the New*, 1923, p. 95; T. S. Eliot, *Selected Essays*, 3rd ed., 1951, p. 169. See also R. C. Bald, 'The Sources of Middleton's City Comedies', *JEGP*, XXXIII (1934), 373–87.
[24] For the social background in relation to Middleton's comedy, see K. M. Lynch, *The Social Mode of Restoration Comedy*, New York, 1926, pp. 24–8, and L. C. Knights, *Drama and Society in the Age of Jonson*, 1937, pp. 256–69.

immorality ... the apotheosis of irreverence, wantonness, and
filth'. And M. L. Hunt bewailed the fact that Middleton, 'concentrat-
ing his great gifts upon the evil and the unclean', had 'carried the
comedy of mud to the greatest length'. [25]

But this point of view overlooks completely the morality implicit
in Middleton's ironic attitude. M. C. Bradbrook writes in discussing
A Trick that

> Although the accent of judgment is heard in Jonson's plays from
> beginning to end ... in Middleton the silent judgment is provided
> by weight of irony—by all that is left unsaid. [26]

Irony is indeed the most characteristic and distinctive element of
Middleton's style in *A Trick*, so pervasive as to be far more than an
incidental technique: it is the essence of his point of view. It is
impossible to illustrate the superb structural irony of the play without
summarising the entire plot. The whole action leads up to Hoard's
final rueful words, 'Who seem most crafty prove oft times most fools'
—the controlling idea of nearly all the early Middleton comedies
which concern themselves with the sharking life of London. In a
world peopled almost entirely by vicious characters, the necessity for
explicit condemnation goes—we can watch, in this play, greed bring
about its own downfall as rogue cheats rogue and dog eats dog. The
idea is essentially a moral one, though Middleton does not, to his
credit, handle it crudely. He is greatly helped by the intrigue
formula on which the plot is built. With its cycle of deception and
self-deception, exposure and mortification between rogue and rogue
or between rogue and gull, with its manipulators and manipulated,
the intrigue plot is the perfect vehicle for conveying Middleton's
satiric vision of a world where almost the only passion is greed, the
greatest gift cunning, where 'there are few sheer fools' and 'all at
least aspire to some degree of knavery'.[27] In short, the formal nature
of the intrigue in *A Trick* makes the thematic point.

The larger reversals of the plot are reinforced by smaller details

[25] A. Symons, 'Middleton and Rowley', *Cambridge History of English
Literature*, 1932, vi, 63; L. B. Wright, *Middle Class Culture in Elizabethan
England*, Chapel Hill, 1935, p. 652; Knights, *op. cit.*, p. 266; A. Harbage,
Shakespeare and the Rival Traditions, New York, 1952, pp. 190 and 196;
C. M. Gayley, ed., *Representative English Comedies*, New York, 1914, iii,
xxiii–xxiv; M. L. Hunt, *Thomas Dekker*, New York, 1911, pp. 92–3.
[26] *op. cit.*, p. 157.
[27] M. C. Bradbrook, *op. cit.*, p. 157. To put the point differently, the intrigue
plot seems particularly appropriate because Middleton 'interests himself
not so much in folly as in vice, not so much in fopperies and affectations as
in rackets and cheats' (S. Schoenbaum, *Middleton's Tragedies*, New York,
1955, p. 167).

which help to keep alert the sense of irony and detachment. For instance, in the tavern from which he is to steal away the 'widow', Hoard asks if any lady has come in, to be told that only Mistress Florence has done so:

HOARD
>What is that Florence? a widow?

DRAWER
>Yes, a Dutch widow.

HOARD
>How?

DRAWER
>That's an English drab, sir; give your worship good morrow.
>[*Exit*]

HOARD
>A merry knave, i'faith! I shall remember a Dutch widow the
>longest day of my life. (III. iii, 12–18)

Later, the dying Dampit seems to mishear the complacent Hoard's announcement of his marriage to 'a rich widow', and repeats incredulously 'A Dutch widow?' And even this does not exhaust the ironic possibilities—Dampit is quick to seize on the innuendo in the widow's name: 'Medler? She keeps open house' (IV. v, 142). The bawdy remark is not gratuitous, as it refers again to the real status of the 'widow'. Finally Hoard is disabused, and his initial words on Dutch widows take on a new and appalling meaning for him:

>Out, out! I am cheated; infinitely cozened! . . . A Dutch widow, a
>Dutch widow, a Dutch widow! (V. ii, 96–8)

Similarly, Lucre praises his house as a sort of superior brothel, where young men can force advantageous matches for themselves— it is 'a very Cole Harbour!' (II. i, 237). Later, however, when the host reports that Hoard has carried the courtesan off to Cole Harbour, Lucre bursts out 'The devil's sanctuary!' (III. iii, 108). Both of these ironies have a 'delayed' effect; others are immediately obvious, like Lucre's complacent aside, 'a simple country fellow', when being completely fooled by the host (II. i, 58), or the courtesan's disarmingly helpless 'The world is so deceitful', as she draws the net tighter round the canny Hoard (III. i, 200). Constantly throughout the play, ordinary language is thus imbued with significance and charged with double meanings.[28] The ironic tone never falters, providing a point of amused detachment from which the morality of the action can be surveyed.

[28] This use of language, relying on pun, innuendo and *doubles entendres*, is also a major feature of Middleton's mature tragic style. See C. Ricks, 'The Moral and Poetic Structure of *The Changeling*', *EC*, X (1960), 290–306, and 'Word Play in *Women Beware Women*', *RES*, XII (1961), 238–50.

In this ironic context, further, there is criticism in the very silence with which the characters accept the unwritten laws of their mercenary society. The absence of explicit moral statement in the play invites such a statement from the audience. Middleton's pervasive irony calls forth the moral response, and the fulminations of Gayley and others against the kind of world he depicts could, in one sense, be taken as a definitive proof of the success of his indirect satiric technique.

Middleton's irony in general derives from situation, and the characters are measured (explicitly, anyway) by intellectual rather than moral standards—'Who seem most crafty prove oft times most fools'. His irony is, however, occasionally and unobtrusively dependent upon a clearly ethical frame of reference. For instance, he puts terms like *conscience* and *goodness* into the mouths of characters for whom such concepts have no real meaning. Lucre cheats the young heir 'as his conscience moved him' (I. i, 116–17); later, Hoard upbraids him for over-reaching him in the swindle:

> like a cunning usurer . . . to enter, as it were, at the back door of the purchase? for thou never cam'st the right way by it.
>   (I. iii, 18–21)

Lucre retorts angrily 'Hast thou the conscience to tell me so, without any impeachment to thyself?' But the truth is that both are 'impeached' by the word *conscience*, as is Witgood, urging the courtesan to marry Hoard—' 'twould ease my conscience well to see thee well bestowed' (III. i, 113–14), an idea he returns to with overt cynicism at the end of the play when he apologises to the stricken Hoard:

> Alas, sir, I was pricked in conscience to see her well bestowed, and where could I bestow her better than upon your pitiful worship?
>   (V. ii, 146–8)[29]

Further, there is the debasement of terms like *honour, justice* and *credit*[30] by Lucre, Hoard and their gentlemen friends. Hoard thanks his gentlemen for their help in his successful mercenary wooing, and one of them replies ' 'Tis for our credits now to see't well ended.' Hoard responds with words which show that for him everything is measured on a monetary scale of values:

[29] The word also is used with ironic overtones at I. i, 9, IV. ii, 48, 54, 81, and 91, IV. iv, 266.
Goodness in the play generally means simply *money*—see I. ii, 37, II. i, 188, III. i, 117.
[30] Middleton plays continually and cleverly on *credit* (= reputation, good name) and *credit* in its monetary sense. The best example of the resultant irony is the gentlemen's 'We'll pawn our credits, widow', at IV. i, 76; but see also II. i, 226–7, III. i, 233, IV. i, 39, IV. iv, 273.

'Tis for your honours, gentlemen; nay, look to't;
Not only in joy, but I in wealth excel.   (III. i, 234–5)

The thwarted Lucre is consoled by one of his friends:

No more, good sir, it is a wrong to us,
To see you injured; in a cause so just
We'll spend our lives, but we will right our friends.
(III. iii, 112–14)

and he leaves Witgood with the righteous words

Nephew, take comfort; a just cause is strong.   (III. iii, 116)

Middleton also places his action, however ironically and tenuously, within the morality framework of the prodigal play, and it has already been pointed out (p. xxiv above) how righteously Lucre and Hoard react to Witgood's prodigality. This sort of indirect moral commentary, by the placing of indignantly righteous speeches in the mouths of corrupt characters, finds its most obviously ironic expression in Hoard's condemnation of Lucre to the widow (III. i, 178–83), but other instances may be easily found in the play.

The usurers of the play are constantly associated with devils. The 'Old One' of the title refers to Satan as well as to Lucre, and the word applied to each other most often by Lucre and Hoard, and to them by others, *adversary*, is a synonym for the devil.[31] Dampit and Gulf are 'two the most prodigious rascals that ever slipped into the shape of men' (I. iv, 5–6). Dampit lies 'like the devil in chains' (IV. v, 6) and Gulf is 'the little dive-dapper of damnation' and 'great Lucifer's little vicar' (IV. v, 126, 159). The creditors are also called devils (IV. iii, 61). Middleton never allows any deepening of the colloquial tone of most of these references, of course, but the impulse to denounce vice is clearly present. The ironic strength of the play, however, depends on his almost total suppression of the overtly didactic tendency.

It has been argued, however, that in the scenes concerning Dampit Middleton's controlled attitude of detachment falters, and an inharmonious didactic tone is sounded. When we last see him, Dampit is apparently dying of drink, and Lamprey comments:

Note but the misery of this usuring slave: here he lies, like a noisome dunghill, full of the poison of his drunken blasphemies, and they to whom he bequeaths all grudge him the very meat that feeds him, the very pillow that eases him. Here may a usurer behold his end. What profits it to be a slave in this world, and a devil i' th' next?
(IV. v, 54–9)

---

[31] *OED*, *s.v.* 1. The play's title is proverbial (see Tilley, W149); and for *old one = devil*, see *OED* under *old*, 9.

Of this, R. B. Parker writes[32] that while Dampit's greed is basically no different from Hoard's or Lucre's,

> the virulence of the attack on him is remarkable. Unless there was some untraced personal satire involved, it provides a clue to a side of Middleton obscured by the neatness of the main plot: it appears to have been used as a safety-valve for disgust.

However, such an interpretation overlooks the obvious comic gusto in Middleton's presentation of Dampit throughout the play. This gusto is indicated in Dampit's exuberant, almost incoherent, use of language. He 'spouts', like the beer and sack he constantly calls for, particularly in his account of his rise to riches (I. iv, 41–68), and in the broadside he directs at Gulf:

> Why, thou rogue of universality, do not I know thee? Thy sound is like the cuckoo, the Welsh ambassador; thou cowardly slave, that offers to fight with a sick man when his weapon's down! Rail upon me in my naked bed? Why, thou great Lucifer's little vicar, I am not so weak but I know a knave at first sight. Thou inconscionable rascal! thou that goest upon Middlesex juries, and will make haste to give up thy verdict, because thou wilt not lose thy dinner, are you answered?   (IV. v, 155–63)

The sheer energy of Dampit's speech, his infectious self-delight in even his drunkenness, must qualify the suggestion that Middleton's attitude is one of 'disgust' (though, of course, Dampit's activities are condemned). Dampit's vice is so straightforward and self-proclaimed that even Witgood, who has been 'nibbled . . . finely' by the old rogue, can say with a hint of admiration, and perhaps of affection, 'Ah, thou'rt a mad old Harry!' (I. iv, 71). Further, Lamprey's moralising comment is an isolated one, especially as regards its tone.

Certainly some 'explanation' for the three Dampit scenes is needed. On the level of intrigue, their connection with the main action is virtually non-existent. To construct a thematic link by taking Dampit as a kind of inflated type of all the sharks of the play, is to distort his obviously minor function and there are difficulties in squaring such a reading with the basically 'realistic' method of the play. Editors have tried to account for this inorganic excrescence on the highly organised plot of the main action by suggesting that Dampit is modelled on a real person (Sampson, p. 17) or is a part written in for a special actor (Spencer, p. 982). This, while possible, is improbable: no clinching evidence has so far come to light; the treatment of the various kinds of idiosyncrasy associated with Dampit in speech, clothes and general behaviour obviously owes a lot to Jonson's humours comedy; and the broad, inflated characterisation

[32] *art. cit.*, p. 188.

is similar to that of Tangle, a 'humorous' lawyer in an earlier Middleton play, *The Phoenix*.

The main reason for dissatisfaction with these theories about the Dampit scenes is that they both suggest a lapse in artistic control hard to credit in the context. One is reluctant to believe that the dispassionate Middleton grew suddenly enraged at the vices he was presenting, or that he would have risked the symmetry of his plot to gratify either a personal grudge or an actor's talent. The exaggeration of these three scenes may, in fact, have been deliberate. Middleton, as we have seen, wants to suggest that the fantastic situations and attitudes of his main action are natural and normal. The extravagant presence of Dampit, the typical stage usurer and lawyer, with his insatiable appetite for alcohol, serves to emphasise by contrast the normality and even, in a curious way, the respectability of Lucre and Hoard. Nevertheless, too much attention is undoubtedly given to Dampit; but an awareness of the comic gusto of the scenes, and of the effect of 'realism' they impart, by contrast, to the main action, may help to make them seem more palatable than they have been to most critics of the play.

Dampit's distinctive mode of utterance also marks him off from the other characters of *A Trick*, in that his highly coloured and syntactically disordered speech places him in the mode of Jonson's linguistic satire, where the linguistic traits of any one character are often as narrowly obsessive as his 'humour'.[33] By contrast with either Jonson's or Shakespeare's prose style, Middleton's is on the whole plain and colloquial, as befits the basically 'realistic' technique and Middleton's ironic aim, which is to stress the ordinariness of vice.

It is hard to illustrate the colloquial, non-metaphoric nature of Middleton's style save in a negative way. Thus, we do not find repeated patterns of images, as in a Shakespearian play, and though it would be wrong to imply that the language had no metaphoric content, it is true that images are rarely *elaborated* and developed, except in a punning kind of way.[34] Striking images, like Witgood's in I. i, 97–9 where he says he will 'pour the sweet circumstance into his ear, which shall have the gift to turn all the wax to honey', are the exception rather than the rule; and in the play figurative language usually has an ironic function, as here, where the bombast makes Hoard's anger ridiculous:

Shall my adversary thus daily affront me, ripping up the old wound

---

[33] See J. A. Barish, *Ben Jonson and the Language of Prose Comedy*, Cambridge, Mass., 1960.
[34] E.g., I. i, 53–8, IV. v, 76–8 and V. ii, 149–52.

of our malice, which three summers could not close up? into
which wound the very sight of him drops scalding lead instead of
balsamum.   (I. iii, 3–6)

The most obvious characteristic of the colloquial style which is the
staple of the play's language is the speed of its movement, its
tumbling energy. This is particularly true of the speech of Witgood,
and can be seen in his opening soliloquy for example, and in the
following, where the impatient exclamation and the parenthetical
phrases contrive to give the convincing impression of a mind fast at
work:

Mass, that's true; the jest will be of some continuance. Let me see;
horses now, a bots on 'em! Stay, I have acquaintance with a mad
host, never yet bawd to thee; I have rinsed the whoreson's gums in
mull-sack many a time and often; put but a good tale into his ear
now, so it come off cleanly, and there's horse and man for us, I dare
warrant thee.   (I. i, 65–70)

This realistically capricious speech is not confined to Witgood and
the rapidity of much of the dialogue accords well with the frenetic
double-crossing of the intrigue.

The linguistic techniques of the play are not unsubtle, however,
not merely concerned with giving an impression of realism and haste.
It has already been shown how ironic situations imbue ordinary
words with a vigorous strength and point. The subtlety and force
of this cannot be illustrated out of context. We have also seen how
skilfully and restrainedly Middleton uses words which establish
an ethical frame of reference.

Finally, in connection with the linguistic mode of the play, we
might notice Middleton's very clever use of verse. In this 'realistic'
prose context, verse will obviously seem highly artificial (though it
is true that in this play Middleton's verse generally shares all the
raciness of the prose, often exceeding ten syllables). His use of verse
is another way, in fact, of undercutting any heavily moral response.
Thus Hoard and Lucre upbraid each other's villainy in verse, the
courtesan plays the demure and innocent widow protesting her
horror at the ways of the world in verse, and Witgood pledges his
good faith and loyalty to his creditors in verse. In all these cases,
verse functions as a means of burlesquing everything that is being
said. (With Witgood and the courtesan the burlesque is conscious.)
The interaction of prose and verse in this way is very effective,
emphasising the obliquity of the moral approach. That Middleton
intended the burlesque effect is demonstrated conclusively by
Witgood's apostrophe to his mortgage (IV. ii, 87–92), and the
'reformation' speeches (V. ii, 153–91), where rhymed couplets, using

either four or five stressed lines, supplement the ironic tone.[35]

A Trick to Catch the Old One is generally regarded as the most distinctive of Middleton's early comedies, and, with *A Chaste Maid in Cheapside*, as one of the most distinguished of all his plays. Dyce considers *A Trick* one of the most perfect of the comedies. Bullen heartily endorses Langbaine's 'brief but emphatic judgement that "this is an excellent old play"'. Swinburne thought it 'by far the best play Middleton had yet written, and one of the best he ever wrote', and T. S. Eliot named it as one of the greatest comedies of a 'great comic writer'.[36] Disagreement has been rare, and usually arises from misinterpretations of Middleton's realism and moral stance.

[35] Some of these points are discussed by W. Creizenach, *English Drama in the Age of Shakespeare*, 1916, p. 322, and by M. Crane, *Shakespeare's Prose*, Chicago, 1951, pp. 53–4.

[36] See Ellis, i, xii–xiii, and T. S. Eliot, *op. cit.*, p. 162.

NOTE ON THE TEXT

IT IS most probable that the copy for Q1 was the author's foul papers or a fair copy of these which Middleton made for sale to the company. It is at any rate unlikely that the play was printed from an acting copy. The scarcity of stage directions (especially of those for entrances), the permissive and sometimes inconsistent nature of the existing stage directions, and the extensive use of mere numbers for speech prefixes, are good signs that the play was printed from an authorial draft. More positively, the spelling and punctuation of Q1 exemplify many of Middleton's habits as they have been established by studies of the MSS of *A Game at Chess* as well as by detailed investigation of the printed texts of his early unaided work and by comparison of these with the habits of his contemporary dramatists.[37]

The fourteen extant copies of the first edition have been collated. Greg's list (*Bibl. Drama*, i, item 262) is incomplete, as he was unaware of the copies in Yale and in the Bute Collection now in the National Library of Scotland. Marion Linton, in an article in *SB*, XV (1962), did not notice that the Bute copy is defective and that H4 was supplied from a copy of the second edition of 1616. (This is a line-for-line reprint and has no editorial value, though it corrects some of Q1's obvious blunders. Both copies of Q2 in the Bodleian Library, Oxford, have been collated.) The following formes are variant in the existing copies of Q1: outer and inner B and C, inner D, outer and inner E, outer and inner G, and inner H. Press-correction was concerned mainly with the rectifying of obvious mechanical errors and, since a large number of these survive, seems to have been fairly slipshod. This edition incorporates the corrections from the ten variant formes.

As the survival of so many of Middleton's distinctive spellings and punctuation habits seems to indicate, his copy was in general treated faithfully in George Eld's printing shop, but the quarto is obviously a job done with a view to the utmost economy. Initially an attempt was made to set up the play in a manner pleasing to the eye, but from B4^v on the text is extremely crowded. The average

---

[37] See R. C. Bald's edition of *A Game at Chess*, 1929, and G. R. Price, 'The Huntington MS of *A Game at Chess*', *HLQ*, XVII (1953), 83–8; also G. R. Price, 'The Authorship and the Bibliography of *The Revenger's Tragedy*', *Library* (Fifth Series), XV (1960), 262–77, P. B. Murray, *A Study of Cyril Tourneur*, Philadelphia, 1964, pp. 144–89, and C. Hoy, 'The Shares of Fletcher and his Collaborators in the Beaumont and Fletcher Canon (V)', *SB*, XIII (1960), 77–108.

number of lines to a page increases, there are many turn-overs and turn-unders, and white space disappears. Speeches are set continuously and many stage directions are squeezed into the last line of a speech. The attempt to save space may also account for the omission of some of the stage directions and, more probably, for some of the mislineation of verse as prose. Here it should be noted, however, that the compositor may not always have been at fault: Middleton's MS of *A Game at Chess* shows that he was careless about lineation, and his easy movement from verse to prose and *vice versa* may have caused confusion. Further, even the verse of his mature tragedies has a markedly colloquial rhythm. Nevertheless, these allowances made, it still seems likely in view of the other space-saving expedients that some of the mislineation is due to the compositor.

The fact that the play was set by formes may also have some bearing on the crowding of the text. Further, miscalculation in casting off copy could be responsible for the omission of some stage directions[38] or even of lines from the text itself, though it is true that there is little of the obscurity one might expect to result from blunders of this kind. (See, however, II. i, where the absence of a stage direction would be surprising even in an author's draft, and IV. v, 1–4, and note.)

An analysis of the evidence supplied by running titles and recurring pieces of broken type shows that the text was imposed in two skeleton formes. Setting was by formes, and the outer went through the press first. The printing of the major part of Q1 proceeded smoothly and efficiently but there are clear indications that there was a break in composition after the printing of the F gathering, and another interruption after the printing of the G gathering. This tends to confirm the evidence supplied by all the economy measures— that the printing of *A Trick* was a hastily run off job which took second place in Eld's shop to more important work. Despite all this, and despite the fact that it has proved impossible to identify the compositor or compositors who set Q1, it seems clear that Middleton's autograph MS was not corrupted by sophistication or extreme carelessness during the printing process.[39]

In this edition, the spelling of Q1 has been modernised, and speech prefixes and contractions silently regularised and expanded.

[38] C. Hinman, *The Printing and Proof-reading of the First Folio of Shakespeare*, 1963, ii, 508, argues that stage directions were most likely to suffer when a compositor miscalculated.

[39] My conclusions about the composition and printing are confirmed in an article which appeared as this edition was going to press. See G. R. Price, 'The Early Editions of *A Trick to Catch the Old One*', *Library* (Fifth Series), XXII (1967), 205–27.

The punctuation of Q1, which seems to reflect pretty faithfully Middleton's own, is eccentric and would be merely a distraction to the modern reader, so it too has been modernised. Act and scene divisions are those established by Dyce, but the occasional divisions supplied by Q1 are recorded in the notes. Editorial stage directions, and any additions to Q1's stage directions, are enclosed in square brackets. All substantive and semi-substantive departures from copy-text (including alterations in the lineation of Q1) are recorded in the notes.

FURTHER READING

Barker, R. H. *Thomas Middleton*, New York, 1958.
Bradbrook, M. C. *The Growth and Structure of Elizabethan Comedy*, 1955.
Dunkel, W. D. *The Dramatic Technique of Thomas Middleton in his Comedies of London Life*, Chicago, 1925.
Eliot, T. S. 'Thomas Middleton', in *Selected Essays*, 3rd edition, 1951.
Ellis-Fermor, U. M. *The Jacobean Drama*, 1936.
Knights, L. C. *Drama and Society in the Age of Jonson*, 1937.
Parker, R. B. 'Middleton's Experiments with Comedy and Judgement', *Stratford-upon-Avon Studies*, edd. Brown and Harris, I (1960), 179-199.
Price, G. R. 'The Early Editions of *A Trick to Catch the Old One*,' *Library* (Fifth Series), XXII (1967), 205-227.
Schoenbaum, S. '*A Chaste Maid in Cheapside* and Middleton's City Comedy', *Studies in the English Renaissance Drama in Memory of K. J. Holzknecht*, edd. J. W. Bennett, O. Cargill, and V. Hall, Jr., New York, 1959, pp. 287–309.

A
Tricke to Catch the
Old-one.

As it hath beene often in Action, both
at Paules, and the Black-
Fryers.

*Presented before his Maiestie on
New-yeares night last.*

Compofde by T.M.

AT LONDON
Printed by *G: E.* and are to be sold by *Henry Rockytt,*
*at the long shop in the Poultrie vnder
the Dyall.* 1608,

[DRAMATIS PERSONAE .

THEODORUS WITGOOD
PECUNIUS LUCRE, *his uncle*
WALKADINE HOARD
ONESIPHORUS HOARD, *his brother*
LIMBER ⎫
KIX ⎬ *friends to* HOARD
LAMPREY ⎭
SPITCHCOCK
HARRY DAMPIT ⎫ *usurers*
GULF ⎭
SAM FREEDOM, *son to* LUCRE'S WIFE
MONEYLOVE
HOST
SIR LANCELOT

GEORGE, *servant to* LUCRE
ARTHUR, *servant to* HOARD

CREDITORS, GENTLEMEN, DRAWER,
  VINTNER, BOY, SCRIVENER,
  SERVANTS, SERGEANTS, *etc.*

COURTESAN
WIFE *to* LUCRE
NIECE *to* HOARD
LADY FOXSTONE
AUDREY, *servant to* DAMPIT

Scene: *A Leicestershire town* (I. i and I. ii),
then London]

3

[Act I, Scene i]

Enter WITGOOD, *a Gentleman, solus*

WITGOOD

All's gone! still thou'rt a gentleman, that's all; but a poor
one, that's nothing. What milk brings thy meadows forth
now? Where are thy goodly uplands and thy downlands? All
sunk into that little pit, lechery. Why should a gallant pay
but two shillings for his ordinary that nourishes him, and   5
twenty times two for his brothel that consumes him?
But where's Long-acre? in my uncle's conscience, which is
three years' voyage about; he that sets out upon his
conscience never finds the way home again—he is either
swallowed in the quicksands of law-quillets, or splits upon   10
the piles of a *praemunire*; yet these old fox-brained and
ox-browed uncles have still defences for their avarice, and
apologies for their practices, and will thus greet our follies:

He that doth his youth expose
To brothel, drink, and danger,   15
Let him that is his nearest kin
Cheat him before a stranger.

And that's his uncle, 'tis a principle in usury. I dare not visit
the city: there I should be too soon visited by that horrible
plague, my debts, and by that means I lose a virgin's love,   20

5 *ordinary* meal in an eating-house or tavern
7 *Long-acre* term applied generally to any estate
7 *conscience* regard for the dictates of conscience
10 *law-quillets* legal subtleties or quibbles
11 *praemunire* a sheriff's writ
12 *ox-browed* cuckolded (or stupid—cf. V. ii, 193)
12 *still* always

4 *little . . . lechery.* Cf. Coverdale's Bible (1535), *Prov.* xxii. 14, 'The
  mouth of an harlot is a depe pytt.'
4–6 *Why . . . him?* Cf. Dekker and Webster's *Westward Ho!,* 1604:
  'Your Farmers that would spend but three pence on his [*sic*] ordinarie,
  would lauish halfe a Crowne on his Leachery' (Bowers, ii, III. iii,
  15–16). Witgood's expensive ordinary would be in keeping with his
  status as a gallant.
7–11 Lucre's lack of compunction is compared to the ocean in its bound-
  lessness; to be dependent on his finer feelings is like making a long and
  dangerous voyage which must end in shipwreck. See III. i, 183, where
  the same metaphor is used.

5

her portion and her virtues. Well, how should a man live now,
that has no living; hum? Why, are there not a million of men
in the world, that only sojourn upon their brain, and make
their wits their mercers; and am I but one amongst that
million and cannot thrive upon't? Any trick, out of the   25
compass of law, now would come happily to me.

Enter COURTESAN

COURTESAN
My love.
WITGOOD
My loathing! hast thou been the secret consumption of my
purse? and now com'st to undo my last means, my wits? wilt
leave no virtue in me, and yet thou never the better?   30
Hence, courtesan, round-webbed tarantula,
That dryest the roses in the cheeks of youth!
COURTESAN
I have been true unto your pleasure, and all your lands
thrice racked, was never worth the jewel which I prodigally
gave you, my virginity;   35
Lands mortgaged may return and more esteemed,
But honesty, once pawned, is ne'er redeemed.
WITGOOD
Forgive: I do thee wrong
To make thee sin and then to chide thee for't.
COURTESAN
I know I am your loathing now: farewell.   40
WITGOOD
Stay, best invention, stay.
COURTESAN
I that have been the secret consumption of your purse, shall I
stay now to undo your last means, your wits? Hence
courtesan, away!

23–4 *make . . . mercers* rely on their wits to keep up appearances
25–6 *out . . . law* not punishable by law
31 ed. prose in Qq
31 *round-webbed* 'referring to the hooped farthingale?' (Sampson)
34 *racked* rented at excessively high rates
37 *honesty* chastity
41 *invention* device (referring to her as the instrument for his scheme)

31 *tarantula.* The spider traditionally 'turns all into Excrement and
Venom' (Swift, *The Battle of the Books*). Cf. Donne's 'The spider love,
which transubstantiates all' ('Twicknam Garden'), and IV. v, 26.

WITGOOD
I prithee, make me not mad at my own weapon, stay (a thing   45
few women can do, I know that, and therefore they had need
wear stays); be not contrary. Dost love me? Fate has so cast
it that all my means I must derive from thee.

COURTESAN
From me! Be happy then;
What lies within the power of my performance   50
Shall be commanded of thee.

WITGOOD   Spoke like
An honest drab i'faith; it may prove something.
What trick is not an embryon at first,
Until a perfect shape come over it?

COURTESAN
Come, I must help you, whereabouts left you?   55
I'll proceed.
Though you beget, 'tis I must help to breed.
Speak, what is't? I'd fain conceive it.

WITGOOD
So, so, so; thou shall presently take the name and form upon
thee of a rich country widow, four hundred a year valiant, in   60
woods, in bullocks, in barns and in rye-stacks; we'll to
London, and to my covetous uncle.

COURTESAN
I begin to applaud thee; our states being both desperate,
they're soon resolute. But how for horses?

WITGOOD
Mass, that's true; the jest will be of some continuance. Let   65
me see; horses now, a bots on 'em! Stay, I have acquaintance
with a mad host, never yet bawd to thee; I have rinsed the
whoreson's gums in mull-sack many a time and often; put

45 *a thing* i.e., to be staid or steadfast
47–8 *Fate . . . thee* run on ed. as new par. Qq
47 *cast* planned
51–4 ed. prose in Qq
60 *valiant* worth
64 *resolute* decided
66 *bots* a common disease of worms, affecting the gums of horses
67 *mad* merry
68 *mull-sack* sack heated, sweetened and spiced

64 *they're.* Q1 they'are. The only instance in this play of the 'Jonsonian'
apostrophe to indicate elision, which other modern editors overlook.
67 *bawd.* As Spencer notes, innkeepers were apt to be procurers. See
I. ii, 17–18.

but a good tale into his ear now, so it come off cleanly, and
there's horse and man for us, I dare warrant thee.   70

COURTESAN
Arm your wits then
Speedily; there shall want nothing in me,
Either in behaviour, discourse or fashion,
That shall discredit your intended purpose.
I will so artfully disguise my wants,   75
And set so good a courage on my state,
That I will be believed.

WITGOOD
Why, then, all's furnished; I shall go nigh to catch that old
fox, mine uncle. Though he make but some amends for my
undoing, yet there's some comfort in't—he cannot otherwise   80
choose (though it be but in hope to cozen me again) but
supply any hasty want that I bring to town with me. The
device well and cunningly carried, the name of a rich widow,
and four hundred a year in good earth, will so conjure up a
kind of usurer's love in him to me, that he will not only desire   85
my presence—which at first shall scarce be granted him,
I'll keep off a' purpose—but I shall find him so officious to
deserve, so ready to supply! I know the state of an old man's
affection so well; if his nephew be poor indeed, why, he lets
God alone with him; but if he be once rich, then he'll be the   90
first man that helps him.

COURTESAN
'Tis right the world; for in these days an old man's love to
his kindred is like his kindness to his wife, 'tis always done
before he comes at it.

WITGOOD
I owe thee for that jest. Begone, here's all my wealth;   95
prepare thyself, away! I'll to mine host with all possible
haste, and with the best art, and most profitable form, pour

69 *cleanly* cleverly, adroitly
71–4 ed. prose in Qq
76 *set . . . state* assume such confidence (or boldness) in the value of
    my estate
79–80 *for my undoing* for ruining me
81 *cozen* cheat
87–8 *officious to deserve* eager to become entitled to reward
89–90 *lets . . . him* leaves it to God to look after him
92 *right . . . world* precisely the way of the world
93 *kindness* love (here in a specifically sexual sense)
95 *owe* am indebted to

the sweet circumstance into his ear, which shall have the gift
to turn all the wax to honey.   [*Exit* COURTESAN]
How now? oh, the right worshipful seniors of our country!   100

[*Enter* ONESIPHORUS HOARD, LIMBER, *and* KIX]

ONESIPHORUS
Who's that?

LIMBER
Oh, the common rioter, take no note of him.

WITGOOD
[*Aside*] You will not see me now; the comfort is,
Ere it be long you will scarce see yourselves.   [*Exit*]

ONESIPHORUS
I wonder how he breathes; h'as consumed all   105
Upon that courtesan!

LIMBER   We have heard so much.

ONESIPHORUS
You have heard all truth. His uncle and my brother
Have been these three years mortal adversaries.
Two old tough spirits, they seldom meet but fight,
Or quarrel when 'tis calmest;   110
I think their anger be the very fire
That keeps their age alive.

LIMBER
What was the quarrel, sir?

 98 *gift* power
100 *now* ed. no Qq
102 *common rioter* notorious profligate
103–10 ed. prose in Qq

100ff. *Onesiphorus, Limber, Kix*. Proper names can be substituted for the
    numerals of Qq's speech headings on the evidence of the following
    lines and of V. ii, 46ff. Onesiphorus, a Puritan name actually in use,
    means 'profit-bearing', with an obvious irony; Kix is a dried up stalk,
    and Limber's name refers ironically to his age. For a full discussion of
    Middleton's nomenclature, see W. Power, 'Middleton's Way with
    Names', *NQ*, New Series VII (1960), 26–29 and ff.

106 *that courtesan*. This easy, familiar reference is of some importance to our
    appreciation of the dénouement. F. S. Boas, *An Introduction to Stuart
    Drama*, 1946, p. 223 writes: 'the disclosure of the widow's real identity
    in the short final act is too forced and abrupt as it comes from . . .
    Onesiphorus . . . Limber and Kix . . . who have merely caught sight
    of the courtesan for a moment in the opening scene'. But, as Middleton
    deftly indicates here, she was evidently a figure of some notoriety in
    the town: the recognition and horror in V. ii is very adequately pre-
    pared for.

ONESIPHORUS

Faith, about a purchase, fetching over a young heir; Master
Hoard, my brother, having wasted much time in beating   115
the bargain, what did me old Lucre, but as his conscience
moved him, knowing the poor gentleman, stepped in
between 'em and cozened him himself.

LIMBER

And was this all, sir?

ONESIPHORUS

This was e'en it, sir; yet for all this I know no reason but the   120
match might go forward betwixt his wife's son and my niece;
what though there be a dissension between the two old men,
I see no reason it should put a difference between the two
younger; 'tis as natural for old folks to fall out, as for young
to fall in! A scholar comes a-wooing to my niece: well, he's   125
wise, but he's poor; her son comes a-wooing to my niece: well,
he's a fool, but he's rich—

LIMBER

Ay, marry, sir?

ONESIPHORUS

Pray, now, is not a rich fool better than a poor philosopher?

LIMBER

One would think so, i'faith!   130

ONESIPHORUS

She now remains at London with my brother, her second
uncle, to learn fashions, practise music; the voice between
her lips, and the viol between her legs; she'll be fit for a
consort very speedily. A thousand good pound is her
portion; if she marry, we'll ride up and be merry.   135

KIX

A match, if it be a match!   *Exeunt*

114 *purchase* profit (from a shady deal)
114 *fetching over* cheating
115–16 *beating . . . bargain* haggling
125 *fall in* make up after a quarrel
125 *A scholar* Moneylove (see I. iii)
134 *consort* pun on (i) concert (ii) husband
136 *A match* agreed

---

114 *purchase.* The word was closely associated with the world of coney-
catching. Robert Greene, in *A Notable Discovery of Cozenage*, 1591,
glosses some of the sharpers' most common expressions: 'The partie
that taketh vp the Connie, the Setter . . . The monie that is won,
Purchase' (Grosart, x, 38). The fetching over of a young heir—or any
rich young fool—is the most common motif of coney-catching literature.

[Act I, Scene ii]

Enter at one door, WITGOOD, *at the other,* HOST

WITGOOD
  Mine host!
HOST
  Young Master Witgood.
WITGOOD
  I have been laying all the town for thee.
HOST
  Why, what's the news, bully Hadland?
WITGOOD
  What geldings are in the house, of thine own? Answer me to   5
  that first.
HOST
  Why, man, why?
WITGOOD
  Mark me what I say: I'll tell thee such a tale in thine ear,
  that thou shalt trust me spite of thy teeth, furnish me with
  some money, willy-nilly, and ride up with me myself *contra*   10
  voluntatem et professionem.
HOST
  How? Let me see this trick, and I'll say thou hast more art
  than a conjuror.
WITGOOD
  Dost thou joy in my advancement?
HOST
  Do I love sack and ginger?   15
WITGOOD
  Comes my prosperity desiredly to thee?
HOST
  Come forfeitures to a usurer, fees to an officer, punks to an
  host, and pigs to a parson desiredly? why, then, la.

3 *laying* searching   4 *bully* a familiar term of address
4 *Hadland* a humorous title for one who formerly owned land and
  has lost it. Cf. 'Lackland'
9 *spite . . . teeth* despite yourself
10–11 *contra . . . professionem* against your will and profession
12 *How* What? (exclamation of surprise)
17 *punks* prostitutes. Cf. I. i, 67
18 *pigs . . . parson* proverbial reference to the time when the parson
  collected his tithe in kind
18 *la* exclamation, meaningless in itself, usually accompanying an
  emphatic statement

WITGOOD

Will the report of a widow of four hundred a year, boy, make
thee leap, and sing, and dance, and come to thy place again?   20

HOST

Wilt thou command me now? I am thy spirit; conjure me
into any shape.

WITGOOD

I ha' brought her from her friends, turned back the horses
by a sleight; not so much as one amongst her six men, goodly
large yeomanly fellows, will she trust with this her purpose: 25
by this light, all unmanned, regardless of her state, neglectful
of vainglorious ceremony, all for my love; oh, 'tis a fine little
voluble tongue, mine host, that wins a widow.

HOST

No, 'tis a tongue with a great T, my boy, that wins a widow.

WITGOOD

Now sir, the case stands thus: good mine host, if thou lov'st   30
my happiness, assist me.

HOST

Command all my beasts i'th' house.

WITGOOD

Nay, that's not all neither; prithee take truce with thy joy,
and listen to me. Thou know'st I have a wealthy uncle i'th'
city, somewhat the wealthier by my follies; the report of this   35
fortune, well and cunningly carried, might be a means to
draw some goodness from the usuring rascal; for I have put
her in hope already of some estate that I have either in land
or money: now, if I be found true in neither, what may I
expect but a sudden breach of our love, utter dissolution of   40
the match, and confusion of my fortunes for ever?

HOST

Wilt thou but trust the managing of thy business with me?

WITGOOD

With thee? Why, will I desire to thrive in my purpose? Will I
hug four hundred a year, I that know the misery of nothing?
Will that man wish a rich widow, that has never a hole to   45
put his head in? With thee, mine host? Why, believe it, sooner
with thee than with a covey of counsellors!

HOST

Thank you for your good report, i'faith, sir, and if I stand
you not in stead, why then let an host come off *hic et haec*

29 *great* capital
49–50 *hic ... hostis* 'a pun on the meaning *host* and *enemy* is intended'
    (Baskervill), though the phrase does not have any literal import

hostis, a deadly enemy to dice, drink, and venery. Come,   50
where's this widow?
WITGOOD
Hard at Park End.
HOST
I'll be her serving-man for once.
WITGOOD
Why, there we let off together, keep full time; my thoughts
were striking then just the same number.   55
HOST
I knew't; shall we then see our merry days again?
WITGOOD
Our merry nights—which never shall be more seen.   *Exeunt*

[Act I, Scene iii]

Enter at several doors, old LUCRE, *and old* HOARD,
Gentlemen [i.e. LAMPREY, SPITCHCOCK, SAM FREEDOM
and MONEYLOVE] *coming between them, to pacify 'em*

LAMPREY
Nay, good Master Lucre, and you, Master Hoard, anger is
the wind which you're both too much troubled withal.
HOARD
Shall my adversary thus daily affront me, ripping up the
old wound of our malice, which three summers could not
close up? into which wound the very sight of him drops   5
scalding lead instead of balsamum.
LUCRE
Why, Hoard, Hoard, Hoard, Hoard, Hoard; may I not pass
in the state of quietness to mine own house? Answer me to
that, before witness, and why? I'll refer the cause to honest,
even-minded gentlemen, or require the mere indifferences   10
of the law to decide this matter. I got the purchase, true;
was't not any man's case? Yes. Will a wise man stand as a

50 *venery* lechery
52 *Hard* near-by
52 *Park End* probably no particular locality is intended
s.d. *several* different
10 *indifferences* impartiality. The plural form is historically correct
12–13 *as . . . bawd* as a third party

---

s.d. *Lamprey, Spitchcock*. A lamprey was an eel-like fish, and a spitchcock a
fried eel (see V. ii, 20–22).

bawd, whilst another wipes his nose of the bargain? No, I
answer no in that case.

LAMPREY

Nay, sweet Master Lucre.   15

HOARD

Was it the part of a friend? no, rather of a Jew—mark what I
say—when I had beaten the bush to the last bird, or, as I may
term it, the price to a pound, then like a cunning usurer to
come in the evening of the bargain, and glean all my hopes
in a minute? to enter, as it were, at the back door of the   20
purchase? for thou never cam'st the right way by it.

LUCRE

Hast thou the conscience to tell me so, without any impeachment to thyself?

HOARD

Thou that canst defeat thy own nephew, Lucre, lap his lands
into bonds, and take the extremity of thy kindred's forfei-   25
tures, because he's a rioter, a wastethrift, a brothel-master,
and so forth—what may a stranger expect from thee, but
vulnera dilacerata, as the poet says, dilacerate dealing?

LUCRE

Upbraid'st thou me with nephew? Is all imputation laid upon
me? What acquaintance have I with his follies? If he riot,   30
'tis he must want it; if he surfeit, 'tis he must feel it; if he
drab it, 'tis he must lie by't; what's this to me?

HOARD

What's all to thee? Nothing, nothing; such is the gulf of thy

13 *wipes his nose* cheats him
16 *Jew* the type of heartlessness on the Elizabethan stage
19 *evening . . . bargain* at the eleventh hour in the chaffering
24 *defeat* dispossess
26 *wastethrift, brothel-master* according to the *OED*, first used by
   Middleton   32 *drab* whore
33 *gulf* instability (literally, voracious belly, a conventional attribute
   of the usurer)

---

17 *beaten . . . bird.* 'One beats the bush and another catches the bird' is
   proverbial, but it is possible that Middleton was here thinking of
   Greene's *Black Book's Messenger*, 1592, where a catalogue of the terms
   of city roguery runs: 'He that drawes the fish to the bait, *the Beater.*
   The Tauerne where they goe, *the Bush.* The foole that is caught, *the
   Bird* . . . The fetching in a Conny, *beating the Bush*' (Grosart, xi, 7).
28 *vulnera dilacerata.* Lacerated wounds. Untraced, and possibly non-
   existent. The comic point is in the inflated language, the pomposity, of
   Hoard's anger.

desire, and the wolf of thy conscience; but be assured, old
Pecunius Lucre, if ever fortune so bless me, that I may be at   35
leisure to vex thee, or any means so favour me, that I may
have opportunity to mad thee, I will pursue it with that
flame of hate, that spirit of malice, unrepressed wrath, that I
will blast thy comforts.

LUCRE
  Ha, ha, ha!   40

LAMPREY
  Nay, Master Hoard, you're a wise gentleman.

HOARD
  I will so cross thee.

LUCRE
  And I thee.

HOARD
  So without mercy fret thee.

LUCRE
  So monstrously oppose thee!   45

HOARD
  Dost scoff at my just anger? Oh, that I had as much power
  as usury has over thee!

LUCRE
  Then thou wouldst have as much power as the devil has over
  thee.

HOARD
  Toad!   50

LUCRE
  Aspic!

HOARD
  Serpent!

LUCRE
  Viper!

SPITCHCOCK
  Nay gentlemen, then we must divide you perforce.

LAMPREY
  When the fire grows too unreasonable hot, there's no better   55
  way than to take off the wood.
                    Exeunt. Manent SAM *and* MONEYLOVE

42 *cross* thwart, oppose
51 *Aspic* asp   56 s.d. *Manent* ed. *Manet* Qq

---

34 *wolf.* Usurers were often likened to wolves: see Sir Thomas Wilson,
  A Discourse upon Usury, 1572, where they are described as 'greedie
  cormoraunte wolfes in deede, that rauyn vp both beaste and man.'

SAM

A word, good signior.

MONEYLOVE

How now, what's the news?

SAM

'Tis given me to understand, that you are a rival of mine in
the love of Mistress Joyce, Master Hoard's niece: say me ay,   60
say me no.

MONEYLOVE

Yes, 'tis so.

SAM

Then look to yourself: you cannot live long. I'm practising
every morning; a month hence I'll challenge you.

MONEYLOVE

Give me your hand upon't; there's my pledge I'll meet you!   65
                 Strikes him.   *Exit*

SAM

Oh, oh!—What reason had you for that, sir, to strike before
the month? You knew I was not ready for you, and that made
you so crank. I am not such a coward to strike again, I
warrant you. My ear has the law of her side for it burns
horribly. I will teach him to strike a naked face, the longest   70
day of his life; 'slid, it shall cost me some money, but I'll
bring this box into the Chancery.   *Exit*

[Act I, Scene iv]

Enter WITGOOD *and the* HOST

HOST

Fear you nothing, sir; I have lodged her in a house of credit,
I warrant you.

WITGOOD

Hast thou the writings?

HOST

Firm, sir.

67 *month* ed. mouth Q1
68 *crank* aggressively cocky
68 *again* back
70 *naked* defenceless, unprotected
72 *box* possibly a pun on *box* meaning (i) blow (ii) case
72 *Chancery* the Lord Chancellor's court, the highest court of
    judicature next to the House of Lords
 3 *writings* the spurious documents presented to Lucre at II. i, 35

[*Enter* DAMPIT *and* GULF, *who talk apart*]

WITGOOD

Prithee, stay, and behold two the most prodigious rascals   5
that ever slipped into the shape of men: Dampit, sirrah, and
young Gulf, his fellow caterpillar.

HOST

Dampit? Sure I have heard of that Dampit.

WITGOOD

Heard of him? Why, man, he that has lost both his ears may
hear of him: a famous infamous trampler of time; his   10
own phrase. Note him well: that Dampit, sirrah, he in the
uneven beard, and the serge cloak, is the most notorious,
usuring, blasphemous, atheistical, brothel-vomiting rascal,
that we have in these latter times now extant, whose first
beginning was the stealing of a masty dog from a farmer's   15
house.

HOST

He looked as if he would obey the commandments well,
when he began first with stealing.

WITGOOD

True. The next town he came at, he set the dogs together
by th' ears.   20

7 *caterpillar* extortioner
10 *trampler* attorney, petty solicitor
15 *masty* mastiff
17 *commandments* ed. commandment Qq
19–20 *set . . . ears* set men at variance (proverbial)

---

4 s.d. Other editors place the entry of Dampit and Gulf at l. 30. Apart
from what seems the physical proof that they enter now, in Witgood's
description of Dampit, surely the scene gains added comic point by
the presence of the two usurers, 'conversing apart' during Witgood's
unflattering comments. This kind of situation is repeated in the play,
in III. i, 121–236, IV. i, 37–95, and IV. iv, 165–75. Dampit's name is
self-explanatory, as the song in IV. v makes quite clear; for Gulf, see
gloss at I. iii, 33.

9 *lost . . . ears.* A legal punishment; hence the implication may be: 'Any
criminal would know of Dampit.'

10 *trampler* With Dampit's later account of his frenetic activity and his
'trashing' and 'trotting' about his business, the accurate descriptiveness
of the cant word (apparently first used by Middleton) becomes clear.

12 *uneven . . . cloak.* This has led some commentators on the play to think
that Dampit is a caricature of a real person, but the unkempt beard and
serge cloak were typical of the poor (see M. C. Linthicum, *Costume in
the Drama of Shakespeare and his Contemporaries*, 1936, p. 89), or, as
here, of those who pretended to poverty.

HOST

A sign he should follow the law, by my faith.

WITGOOD

So it followed, indeed; and being destitute of all fortunes,
staked his masty against a noble, and by great fortune his dog
had the day. How he made it up ten shillings I know not, but
his own boast is that he came to town but with ten shillings in   25
his purse, and now is credibly worth ten thousand pound!

HOST

How the devil came he by it?

WITGOOD

How the devil came he not by it? if you put in the devil once,
riches come with a vengeance. H'as been a trampler of the
law, sir, and the devil has a care of his footmen. The rogue   30
has spied me now: he nibbled me finely once too; a pox
search you—oh, Master Dampit!—the very loins of thee!—
cry you mercy, Master Gulf, you walk so low I promise you
I saw you not, sir!

GULF

He that walks low walks safe, the poets tell us.   35

WITGOOD

[*Aside*] And nigher hell by a foot and a half than the rest of
his fellows.—But, my old Harry!

DAMPIT

My sweet Theodorus!

WITGOOD

'Twas a merry world when thou cam'st to town with ten
shillings in thy purse.   40

DAMPIT

And now worth ten thousand pound, my boy; report it,

23 *noble* a gold coin worth 6s. 8d.
33 *cry . . . mercy* beg your pardon

---

30 *footmen.* Continuing the 'trampling' imagery associated with Dampit's
job.
35 *low.* Witgood had meant that Gulf was of such a low stature (see IV. v,
126, 159) that he had overlooked him. Gulf, however, takes the word as
meaning 'humble', and his penchant for the classics (see IV. v, 149)
causes him to refer obliquely to the idea of the ancient 'poets' that one
avoided the wrath of the gods by living humbly (cf. 3 *Henry VI*, IV. vi,
19–20). Witgood's swift *sotto voce* riposte neatly deflates this piece of
philosophising.
38 *Theodorus* = gift of God. W. Power, 'Middleton's Way with Names',
p. 60, suggests that Witgood's two names, taken together, might be
interpreted as meaning: 'cleverness is God's gift to man'.

Harry Dampit, a trampler of time, say, he would be up in
a morning, and be here with his serge gown, dashed up to
the hams in a cause; have his feet stink about Westminster
Hall, and come home again; see the galleons, the galleasses,   45
the great armadas of the law; then there be hoys and petty
vessels, oars and scullers of the time; there be picklocks of the
time too. Then would I be here, I would trample up and
down like a mule; now to the judges, 'May it please your
reverend-honourable fatherhoods'; then to my counsellor,   50
'May it please your worshipful patience'; then to the
examiner's office, 'May it please your mastership's gentleness'; then to one of the clerks, 'May it please your worshipful lousiness', for I find him scrubbing in his codpiece; then
to the Hall again, then to the chamber again—   55

WITGOOD

And when to the cellar again?

DAMPIT

E'en when thou wilt again! Tramplers of time, motions of
Fleet Street, and visions of Holborn; here I have fees of one,
there I have fees of another; my clients come about me, the

44 *have . . . stink* Cf. III. iv, 68
44–5 *Westminster Hall* where the law courts were held until 1882
45 *galleasses* heavy galleys
46 *hoys* small coasting vessels
47 *oars* rowing boats. Similarly, *scullers* means sculling boats
47 *picklocks* Dampit turns from the officers of the law to its trans-
     gressors, probably his clients
50 *counsellor* the legal advocate
52 *examiner's* function was to take the depositions of witnesses
54 *scrubbing* scratching (because of lice)
54 *codpiece* a bagged appendage to the front of the breeches
57 *motions* puppets or puppet-shows

---

43 *dashed.* Bespattered with mud. Dekker in *News from Hell* (1606) des-
    cribes lawyers' clerks as being 'durtied vp to the hammes with trudging
    vp and downe to get pelfe, and with fishing for gudgeons' (A. B. Grosart,
    ed., *The Non-Dramatic Works of Thomas Dekker*, 5 vols., 1884–86, ii,
    94).
57–8 *motions . . . Holborn.* The precise meaning here is obscure. Perhaps
    we need take it only as another example of Dampit's energetic inco-
    herence. Spencer glosses: 'We tramplers of time move along Fleet
    Street, on our business errands, with the mechanical regularity of
    puppets. You may see us . . . also in Holborn . . . Hence, we are
    visions of Holborn.' These two streets, favourite haunts of sharpers (see
    Greene's *Notable Discovery of Cozenage*, Grosart, x, 15), are mentioned
    in the song which begins IV. v.

fooliaminy and coxcombry of the country; I still trashed and 60
trotted for other men's causes. Thus was poor Harry
Dampit made rich by others' laziness, who, though they
would not follow their own suits, I made 'em follow me with
their purses.

WITGOOD
Didst thou so, old Harry? 65

DAMPIT
Ay, and I soused 'em with bills of charges, i'faith; twenty
pound a year have I brought in for boat-hire, and I never
stepped into boat in my life.

WITGOOD
Tramplers of time!

DAMPIT
Ay, tramplers of time, rascals of time, bull-beggars! 70

WITGOOD
Ah, thou'rt a mad old Harry! Kind Master Gulf, I am bold to
renew my acquaintance.

GULF
I embrace it, sir. *Music.* *Exeunt*

[Act II, Scene i]

Enter LUCRE

LUCRE
My adversary evermore twits me with my nephew, forsooth,
my nephew; why may not a virtuous uncle have a dissolute
nephew? What though he be a brotheller, a wastethrift, a common surfeiter, and, to conclude, a beggar; must sin in him
call up shame in me? Since we have no part in their follies, 5
why should we have part in their infamies? For my strict
hand toward his mortgage, that I deny not, I confess I had an

---

60 *fooliaminy* fools (with *coxcombry*, the first of the many coinages
    Middleton is to put into Dampit's mouth. See also III. iv, 45–6
    and IV. v, 25, 48–9)
60 *trashed* walked or ran through mud and mire
66 *soused* ed. (souc'st Q1 = sauced?) swindled. Cf. modern *soaked*
70 *bull-beggars* hob-goblins, scare-crows
s.d. ed. *Incipit ACT. 2.* Qq
  1 *twits* censures, upbraids

---

73 s.d. *Music.* Particularly popular in the theatres of the boy actors, which
    derived originally from 16th-century choir schools.

uncle's pen'worth: let me see, half in half, true. I saw neither
hope of his reclaiming, nor comfort in his being, and was it
not then better bestowed upon his uncle, than upon one of   10
his aunts?—I need not say bawd, for everyone knows what
'aunt' stands for in the last translation.

                    [*Enter* SERVANT]
Now, sir?
SERVANT
There's a country serving-man, sir, attends to speak with your
worship.   15
LUCRE
I'm at best leisure now; send him in to me. [*Exit* SERVANT]

              Enter HOST *like a serving-man*
HOST
Bless your venerable worship.
LUCRE
Welcome, good fellow.
HOST
[*Aside*] He calls me thief at first sight, yet he little thinks
I am an host!   20
LUCRE
What's thy business with me?
HOST
Faith, sir, I am sent from my mistress to any sufficient
gentleman indeed, to ask advice upon a doubtful point; 'tis
indifferent, sir, to whom I come, for I know none, nor did my
mistress direct me to any particular man, for she's as mere a   25
stranger here as myself; only I found your worship within,
and 'tis a thing I ever loved, sir, to be dispatched as soon
as I can.
LUCRE
[*Aside*] A good blunt honesty, I like him well.—What is thy
mistress?   30
HOST
Faith, a country gentlewoman and a widow, sir. Yesterday

14 SERVANT ed. *Ser.* 2 Qq
18 *good fellow* cant name for a thief
22 *sufficient* well-to-do
31–2 *Yesterday . . . us* we originally intended to leave (London)
   yesterday
_____

8 *uncle's pen'worth.* To 'uncle' was to cheat or swindle. (This represents a
   variation on the cousin-cozen pun: see Introduction, pp. xxi-xxii).

was the first flight of us, but now she intends to stay till a
little term business be ended.

LUCRE

Her name, I prithee?

HOST

It runs there in the writings, sir, among her lands: Widow   35
Medler.

LUCRE

Medler? Mass, have I never heard of that widow?

HOST

Yes, I warrant you, have you, sir; not the rich widow in
Staffordshire?

LUCRE

Cuds me, there 'tis indeed; thou hast put me into memory;   40
there's a widow indeed, ah, that I were a bachelor again!

HOST

No doubt your worship might do much then, but she's
fairly promised to a bachelor already.

LUCRE

Ah, what is he, I prithee?

HOST

A country gentleman too, one whom your worship knows   45
not, I'm sure; h'as spent some few follies in his youth, but
marriage, by my faith, begins to call him home, my mistress
loves him, sir, and love covers faults, you know: one Master
Witgood, if ever you have heard of the gentleman?

LUCRE

Ha? Witgood, say'st thou?   50

HOST

That's his name indeed, sir; my mistress is like to bring him
to a goodly seat yonder—four hundred a year, by my faith.

LUCRE

But, I pray, take me with you.

HOST

Ay, sir?

LUCRE

What countryman might this young Witgood be?   55

HOST

A Leicestershire gentleman, sir.

---

33 *term business* legal matters, transacted during the court terms.
   See III. i, 96 and note
40 *Cuds* a corruption of *God's*
53 *take . . . you* tell me your meaning

LUCRE

    [*Aside*] My nephew, by th' mass, my nephew! I'll fetch out
more of this, i'faith; a simple country fellow, I'll work't out
of him.—And is that gentleman, say'st thou, presently to
marry her?   60

HOST

    Faith, he brought her up to town, sir; h'as the best card in
all the bunch for't, her heart; and I know my mistress will
be married ere she go down; nay, I'll swear that, for she's
none of those widows that will go down first, and be married
after; she hates that, I can tell you, sir.   65

LUCRE

    By my faith, sir, she is like to have a proper gentleman and a
comely; I'll give her that gift!

HOST

    Why, does your worship know him, sir?

LUCRE

    I know him! Does not all the world know him? Can a man of
such exquisite qualities be hid under a bushel?   70

HOST

    Then your worship may save me a labour, for I had charge
given me to enquire after him.

LUCRE

    Enquire of him? If I might counsel thee, thou shouldst never
trouble thyself furder; enquire of him of no more but of me;
I'll fit thee! I grant he has been youthful, but is he not now   75
reclaimed? Mark you that, sir; has not your mistress, think
you, been wanton in her youth? If men be wags, are there not
women wagtails?

HOST

    No doubt, sir.

LUCRE

    Does not he return wisest, that comes home whipped with his   80
own follies?

HOST

    Why, very true, sir.

LUCRE

    The worst report you can hear of him, I can tell you, is that
he has been a kind gentleman, a liberal, and a worthy; who
but lusty Witgood, thrice noble Witgood!   85

63 *go down* to the country; with an obvious *double entendre*
66 *proper* handsome
70 *bushel* the reference is to *Matt.* v. 15
74 *furder* further   78 *wagtails* wantons

HOST

Since your worship has so much knowledge in him, can you
resolve me, sir, what his living might be? My duty binds me,
sir, to have a care of my mistress's estate; she has been ever a
good mistress to me, though I say it. Many wealthy suitors
has she non-suited for his sake; yet, though her love be so   90
fixed, a man cannot tell whether his non-performance may
help to remove it, sir; he makes us believe he has lands and
living.

LUCRE

Who, young Master Witgood? Why, believe it, he has as
goodly a fine living out yonder—what do you call the place?   95

HOST

Nay, I know not, i'faith.

LUCRE

Hum—see, like a beast, if I have not forgot the name—puh!
And out yonder again, goodly grown woods and fair meadows;
pax on't; I can never hit of that place neither.—He? Why,
he's Witgood of Witgood Hall, he an unknown thing!   100

HOST

Is he so, sir? To see how rumour will alter! Trust me, sir,
we heard once he had no lands, but all lay mortgaged to
an uncle he has in town here.

LUCRE

Push! 'tis a tale, 'tis a tale.

HOST

I can assure you, sir, 'twas credibly reported to my mistress. 105

LUCRE

Why, do you think, i'faith, he was ever so simple to mortgage
his lands to his uncle, or his uncle so unnatural to take the
extremity of such a mortgage?

HOST

That was my saying still, sir.

LUCRE

Puh, never think it.   110

90 *non-suited* this pun on the legal and matrimonial meanings of the
   word is used again at III. i, 95
91 *non-performance* failure to fulfil promises
97 *puh* pooh   99 *pax* pox
104 *Push* Pish. The use of this exclamation is one of Middleton's
   trademarks (see also II. i, 227, III. i, 202)
107–8 *take . . . of* exact the full amount on
109 *That . . . still* That was the story I was always told

HOST
  Yet that report goes current.
LUCRE
  Nay, then you urge me: cannot I tell that best that am his
  uncle?
HOST
  How, sir? What have I done!
LUCRE
  Why, how now! In a swoon, man?   115
HOST
  Is your worship his uncle, sir?
LUCRE
  Can that be any harm to you, sir?
HOST
  I do beseech you, sir, do me the favour to conceal it. What a
  beast was I to utter so much! Pray, sir, do me the kindness
  to keep it in; I shall have my coat pulled o'er my ears, an't   120
  should be known; for the truth is, an't please your worship,
  to prevent much rumour and many suitors, they intend to be
  married very suddenly and privately.
LUCRE
  And dost thou think it stands with my judgement to do them
  injury? Must I needs say the knowledge of this marriage   125
  comes from thee? Am I a fool at fifty-four? Do I lack subtlety
  now, that have got all my wealth by it? There's a leash of
  angels for thee: come, let me woo thee; speak, where lie they?
HOST
  So I might have no anger, sir—
LUCRE
  Passion of me, not a jot; prithee, come.   130
HOST
  I would not have it known it came by my means.
LUCRE
  Why, am I a man of wisdom?
HOST
  I dare trust your worship, sir, but I'm a stranger to your

111 *goes current* is in general circulation
112–3 lineation ed. Cannot . . . Vncle Qq as separate line
115 *swoon* ed. Sowne Qq (= swoon, See *OED*, 'sound', v^4.)
118 *you* ed. your Q1
120 *I . . . ears* I will be stripped of my livery (see l. 147 below), i.e., I
    will lose my job   120 *an* if   127 *leash* a set of three
128 *angels* gold coins worth ten shillings each, having on one side the
    figure of St Michael overcoming the dragon
131 HOST ed. *Hostis* Q1

house; and to avoid all intelligencers, I desire your worship's
ear.   135

LUCRE

[*Aside*] This fellow's worth a matter of trust.—Come, sir.
[HOST *whispers to him*] Why, now, thou'rt an honest lad.—
Ah, sirrah nephew!

HOST

Please you, sir, now I have begun with your worship, when
shall I attend for your advice upon that doubtful point? I   140
must come warily now.

LUCRE

Tut, fear thou nothing; tomorrow's evening shall resolve
the doubt.

HOST

The time shall cause my attendance.   *Exit*

LUCRE

Fare thee well.—There's more true honesty in such a country   145
servingman than in a hundred of our cloak companions: I
may well call 'em companions, for since blue coats have been
turned into cloaks, we can scarce know the man from the
master.—George!

[*Enter* GEORGE]

GEORGE

Anon, sir.   150

LUCRE

List hither: [*whispers*]—keep the place secret. Commend
me to my nephew; I know no cause, tell him, but he might
see his uncle.

GEORGE

I will, sir.

LUCRE

And, do you hear, sir, take heed you use him with respect and   155
duty.

GEORGE

[*Aside*] Here's a strange alteration: one day he must be
turned out like a beggar, and now he must be called in like
a knight!   *Exit*

134 *intelligencers* spies
140 *that . . . point* i.e., the nature of Witgood's living
146 *companions* a term of familiarity or contempt

147–8 *blue . . . cloaks.* The blue coat, the traditional livery of the serving man,
    seems to have been discarded at some time in the very early 17th
    century (see M. C. Linthicum, *op. cit.*, p. 27).

LUCRE

Ah, sirrah, that rich widow! four hundred a year! beside, I 160
hear she lays claim to a title of a hundred more. This falls
unhappily that he should bear a grudge to me now, being
likely to prove so rich. What is't, trow, that he makes me a
stranger for? Hum—I hope he has not so much wit to appre-
hend that I cozened him: he deceives me then. Good heaven, 165
who would have thought it would ever have come to this
pass! yet he's a proper gentleman, i'faith, give him his due—
marry, that's his mortgage; but that I never mean to give him.
I'll make him rich enough in words, if that be good; and if it
come to a piece of money I will not greatly stick for't: there 170
may be hope of some of the widow's lands, too, may one day
fall upon me if things be carried wisely.

[*Enter* GEORGE]

Now, sir, where is he?

GEORGE

He desires your worship to hold him excused; he has such
weighty business it commands him wholly from all men.   175

LUCRE

Were those my nephew's words?

GEORGE

Yes, indeed, sir.

LUCRE

[*Aside*] When men grow rich, they grow proud too, I perceive that. He would not have sent me such an answer once
within this twelvemonth; see what 'tis when a man's come   180
to his lands!—Return to him again, sir; tell him his uncle
desires his company for an hour; I'll trouble him but an hour,
say; 'tis for his own good, tell him; and, do you hear, sir, put
'worship' upon him. Go to, do as I bid you; he's like to be a
gentleman of worship very shortly.   185

GEORGE

[*Aside*] This is good sport, i'faith.   *Exit*

LUCRE

Troth, he uses his uncle discourteously now. Can he tell what
I may do for him? Goodness may come from me in a minute,
that comes not in seven year again. He knows my humour;
I am not so usually good; 'tis no small thing that draws   190

161 *title* deed of property   163 *trow* do you suppose
165 *cozened* cheated
165 *he . . . then* he is not the fool I took him for
170 *stick for* grudge   189 *humour* disposition

3—ATTCTOO

kindness from me, he may know that an he will. The chief
cause that invites me to do him most good is the sudden
astonishing of old Hoard, my adversary. How pale his
malice will look at my nephew's advancement! With what a
dejected spirit he will behold his fortunes, whom but last day   195
he proclaimed rioter, penurious makeshift, despised
brothel-master! Ha, ha! 'twill do me more secret joy than my
last purchase, more precious comfort than all these widow's
revenues.

[*Enter* GEORGE]

Now, sir.   200

GEORGE

With much entreaty he's at length come, sir.   [*Exit*]

Enter WITGOOD

LUCRE

Oh, nephew, let me salute you, sir! You're welcome,
nephew.

WITGOOD

Uncle, I thank you.

LUCRE

Y'ave a fault, nephew; you're a stranger here. Well, heaven   205
give you joy!

WITGOOD

Of what, sir?

LUCRE

Hah, we can hear!
You might have known your uncle's house, i'faith,
You and your widow; go to, you were too blame,   210
If I may tell you so without offence.

WITGOOD

How could you hear of that, sir?

LUCRE   Oh, pardon me,
It was your will to have it kept from me,
I perceive now.

WITGOOD

Not for any defect of love, I protest, uncle.   215

198 *purchase* see I. i, 114
201 s.d. *Enter* WITGOOD after l. 200 in Qq
209–11 ed. prose in Qq   213–14 ed. prose in Qq
213 *it kept* so Q1. Most later editions follow Q2's kept it

210 *too blame*. 'In the 16–17th c. the *to* was misunderstood as *too*, and *blame*
was taken as adj. = *blameworthy, culpable*' (*OED*, 'blame', *v.*, 6). See
also l. 260 below.

LUCRE
Oh, 'twas unkindness, nephew! fie, fie, fie.
WITGOOD
I am sorry you take it in that sense, sir.
LUCRE
Puh, you cannot colour it, i'faith, nephew.
WITGOOD
Will you but hear what I can say in my just excuse, sir?
LUCRE
Yes, faith, will I, and welcome.   220
WITGOOD
You that know my danger i'th' city, sir, so well, how great
my debts are, and how extreme my creditors, could not out
of your pure judgement, sir, have wished us hither.
LUCRE
Mass, a firm reason indeed.
WITGOOD
Else, my uncle's house, why 't'ad been the only make-match. 225
LUCRE
Nay, and thy credit.
WITGOOD
My credit? Nay, my countenance. Push, nay, I know, uncle,
you would have wrought it so by your wit you would have
made her believe in time the whole house had been mine.
LUCRE
Ay, and most of the goods too.   230
WITGOOD
La, you there; well, let 'em all prate what they will, there's
nothing like the bringing of a widow to one's uncle's house.
LUCRE
Nay, let nephews be ruled as they list, they shall find their
uncle's house the most natural place when all's done.
WITGOOD
There they may be bold.   235
LUCRE
Life, they may do anything there, man, and fear neither

216 *unkindness* ingratitude. Baskervill glosses 'unnaturalness, forget-
fulness of the relationship due a relative'
227 *countenance* support of my façade (of wealth)
231 *La* see I. ii, 18

232 *uncle's house.* Sampson suggests that this may have been a slang term for
the residence of an 'aunt', i.e. bawd.

beadle nor summoner. An uncle's house! a very Cole Harbour!
Sirrah, I'll touch thee near now: hast thou so much interest
in thy widow that by a token thou couldst presently send for
her?   240

WITGOOD
Troth, I think I can, uncle.

LUCRE
Go to, let me see that!

WITGOOD
Pray command one of your men hither, uncle.

LUCRE
George!

[Enter GEORGE]

GEORGE
Here, sir.   245

LUCRE
Attend my nephew! [WITGOOD *whispers to* GEORGE, *who then
goes out*] [*Aside*] I love a' life to prattle with a rich widow;
'tis pretty, methinks, when our tongues go together; and
then to promise much and perform little—I love that sport
a' life i'faith. Yet I am in the mood now to do my nephew   250
some good, if he take me handsomely.—What, have you
dispatched?

WITGOOD
I ha' sent, sir.

LUCRE
Yet I must condemn you of unkindness, nephew.

WITGOOD
Heaven forbid, uncle!   255

LUCRE
Yes, faith, must I; say your debts be many, your creditors
importunate, yet the kindness of a thing is all, nephew; you
might have sent me close word on't, without the least danger
or prejudice to your fortunes.

237 *summoner* a petty officer whose function was to warn people to
     appear in court
238–9 *interest in* claim on   258 *close* secret

237 *Cole Harbour.* A warren of tenements by the Thames above London
     Bridge. 'It was regarded as a sanctuary where debtors and malefactors
     were safe from the law' (Spencer), and where, as may be inferred from
     III. i, 227–8, marriages could be hastily solemnised. (*Cole* = cheat,
     sharper).

WITGOOD

Troth, I confess it, uncle, I was too blame there; but, indeed,   260
my intent was to have clapped it up suddenly, and so have
broke forth like a joy to my friends, and a wonder to the
world. Beside, there's a trifle of a forty pound matter toward
the setting of me forth; my friends should never have
known on't; I meant to make shift for that myself.   265

LUCRE

How, nephew? let me not hear such a word again, I beseech
you—shall I be beholding to you?

WITGOOD

To me? Alas, what do you mean, uncle?

LUCRE

I charge you upon my love: you trouble nobody but myself.

WITGOOD

Y'ave no reason for that, uncle.   270

LUCRE

Troth, I'll never be friends with you while you live, an you
do.

WITGOOD

Nay, an you say so, uncle, here's my hand, I will not do't.

LUCRE

Why, well said! there's some hope in thee when thou wilt be
ruled; I'll make it up fifty, faith, because I see thee so   275
reclaimed. Peace, here comes my wife with Sam, her
tother husband's son.

[Enter WIFE *and* SAM]

WITGOOD

Good aunt—

SAM

Cousin Witgood! I rejoice in my salute: you're most
welcome to this noble city governed with the sword in the   280
scabbard.

WITGOOD

[*Aside*] And the wit in the pommel—good Master Sam
Freedom, I return the salute.

264 *setting . . . forth* equipping me, fitting me out
267 *beholding* common in early 17th century for *beholden* (see II. i, 313,
    III. i, 71, IV. iv, 54)
277 *tother* a common form of *other*
282 *wit . . . pommel* the amount of wit in the knob on the hilt of a
    sword

LUCRE
By the mass, she's coming; wife, let me see now how thou
wilt entertain her.   285

WIFE
I hope I am not to learn, sir, to entertain a widow; 'tis not so
long ago since I was one myself.

[*Enter* COURTESAN]

WITGOOD
Uncle—

LUCRE
She's come indeed!

WITGOOD
My uncle was desirous to see you, widow, and I presumed   290
to invite you.

COURTESAN
The presumption was nothing, Master Witgood: is this your
uncle, sir?

LUCRE
Marry am I, sweet widow, and his good uncle he shall find
me; ay, by this smack that I give thee, thou'rt welcome.—   295
Wife, bid the widow welcome the same way again.

SAM
[*Aside*] I am a gentleman now too, by my father's occupation,
and I see no reason but I may kiss a widow by my father's
copy; truly, I think the charter is not against it; surely these
are the words: 'The son, once a gentleman, may revel it,   300
though his father were a dauber;' 'tis about the fifteenth
page—I'll to her—
[*Offers to kiss the* COURTESAN, *who repulses him*]

LUCRE
Y'are not very busy now; a word with thee, sweet widow—

SAM
[*Aside*] Coad's nigs! I was never so disgraced, since the hour
my mother whipped me.   305

LUCRE
Beside, I have no child of mine own to care for; she's my

285 *entertain* receive
292 *your* ed. yours Q1
295 *smack* kiss
299 *copy* example
299 *charter* i.e., of one of the trade guilds
301 *dauber* plasterer
304 *Coad's nigs* God's nigs, a meaningless oath

second wife, old, past bearing; clap sure to him, widow; he's
like to be my heir, I can tell you.

COURTESAN

Is he so, sir?

LUCRE

He knows it already, and the knave's proud on't; jolly rich   310
widows have been offered him here i'th' city, great merchants'
wives, and do you think he would once look upon 'em?
Forsooth, he'll none. You are beholding to him i'th' country,
then, ere we could be; nay, I'll hold a wager, widow, if he
were once known to be in town, he would be presently sought   315
after; nay, and happy were they that could catch him first.

COURTESAN

I think so.

LUCRE

Oh, there would be such running to and fro, widow, he
should not pass the streets for 'em; he'd be took up in one
great house or other presently. Fah! they know he has it, and   320
must have it. You see this house here, widow; this house
and all comes to him, goodly rooms, ready furnished, ceiled
with plaster of Paris, and all hung above with cloth of arras.—
Nephew!

WITGOOD

Sir.   325

LUCRE

Show the widow your house; carry her into all the rooms and
bid her welcome.—You shall see, widow. [*Aside to* WITGOOD]
Nephew, strike all sure above an thou beest a good boy—ah!

WITGOOD

Alas, sir, I know not how she would take it.

LUCRE

The right way, I warrant t'ee. A pox, art an ass? Would I   330
were in thy stead! Get you up; I am ashamed of you.—
[*Exeunt* WITGOOD *and* COURTESAN] So, let 'em agree as they
will now; many a match has been struck up in my house a'
this fashion: let 'em try all manner of ways, still there's

315 *presently* immediately
323 *cloth of arras* rich tapestries, in which figures and scenes (often
    Biblical) were woven in colour

323 *above*. All modern editors, with the exception of Spencer, follow Q2's
    about, but it seems more probable that Lucre is referring to the upstairs
    rooms.

nothing like an uncle's house to strike the stroke in. I'll hold   335
my wife in talk a little.—Now, Jinny, your son there goes a-
wooing to a poor gentlewoman but of a thousand portion;
see my nephew, a lad of less hope, strikes at four hundred a
year in good rubbish.

WIFE
Well, we must do as we may, sir.   340

LUCRE
I'll have his money ready told for him again he come down.
Let me see, too;—by th' mass, I must present the widow
with some jewel, a good piece a' plate, or such a device; 'twill
hearten her on well. I have a very fair standing cup, and a
good high standing cup will please a widow above all other   345
pieces.   *Exit*

WIFE
Do you mock us with your nephew?—I have a plot in my
head, son; i'faith, husband, to cross you.

SAM
Is it a tragedy plot, or a comedy plot, good mother?

WIFE
'Tis a plot shall vex him. I charge you, of my blessing, son   350
Sam, that you presently withdraw the action of your love
from Master Hoard's niece.

SAM
How, mother!

WIFE
Nay, I have a plot in my head, i'faith. Here, take this chain of
gold, and this fair diamond; dog me the widow home to her   355
lodging, and at thy best opportunity fasten 'em both upon
her—nay, I have a reach; I can tell you thou art known what
thou art, son, among the right worshipful, all the twelve
companies.

339 *rubbish* land   341 *again* against, i.e. before
344 *standing* ed. stranding Q1 i.e., on a stem or base (but probably
     with a *double entendre*)
353 *How* see I. ii, 12   357 *reach* scheme

335 *to strike the stroke.* Cf. l. 328 above. This may have sexual connotations (cf.
     Titus Andronicus, II. i, 117–18 and 129–31, and Eric Partridge, *Shake-
     speare's Bawdy*, 1947, p. 196). McKerrow's *Nashe*, iii, 122 indicates that a
     striker was a wencher; but the context in which the phrase recurs at
     III. i, 250 suggests that perhaps this is simply a vigorous way of saying
     'to seal up a bargain'.
358–9 *twelve companies.* The twelve merchants' guilds—or unions—in the
     city of London. See V. ii, 22.

SAM
    Truly, I thank 'em for it.   360
WIFE
    He? he's a scab to thee; and so certify her thou hast two
    hundred a year of thyself, beside thy good parts—a proper
    person and a lovely. If I were a widow, I could find it in my
    heart to have thee myself, son; ay, from 'em all.
SAM
    Thank you for your good will, mother, but indeed I had   365
    rather have a stranger; and if I woo her not in that violent
    fashion that I will make her be glad to take these gifts ere I
    leave her, let me never be called the heir of your body.
WIFE
    Nay, I know there's enough in you, son, if you once come
    to put it forth.   370
SAM
    I'll quickly make a bolt or a shaft on't.   *Exeunt*

[Act II, Scene ii]

Enter HOARD *and* MONEYLOVE

MONEYLOVE
    Faith, Master Hoard, I have bestowed many months in the
    suit of your niece, such was the dear love I ever bore to her
    virtues; but since she hath so extremely denied me, I am to
    lay out for my fortunes elsewhere.
HOARD
    Heaven forbid but you should, sir. I ever told you my niece   5
    stood otherwise affected.
MONEYLOVE
    I must confess you did, sir; yet, in regard of my great loss of
    time, and the zeal with which I sought your niece, shall I
    desire one favour of your worship?
HOARD
    In regard of those two, 'tis hard but you shall, sir.   10
MONEYLOVE
    I shall rest grateful. 'Tis not full three hours, sir, since the
    happy rumour of a rich country widow came to my hearing.

361 *scab . . . thee* scoundrel compared to thee
371 *make . . . on't* do it one way or another (proverbial—literally, use
    a thick arrow or a slender one)
  6 *affected* disposed

HOARD
How? a rich country widow?
MONEYLOVE
Four hundred a year landed.
HOARD
Yea?   15
MONEYLOVE
Most firm, sir, and I have learned her lodging; here my suit
begins, sir: if I might but entreat your worship to be a
countenance for me, and speak a good word—for your words
will pass—I nothing doubt but I might set fair for the
widow; nor shall your labour, sir, end altogether in thanks,   20
two hundred angels—
HOARD
So, so, what suitors has she?
MONEYLOVE
There lies the comfort, sir, the report of her is yet but a
whisper, and only solicited by young riotous Witgood,
nephew to your mortal adversary.   25
HOARD
Ha! art certain he's her suitor?
MONEYLOVE
Most certain, sir, and his uncle very industrious to beguile
the widow, and make up the match!
HOARD
So! very good!
MONEYLOVE
Now, sir, you know this young Witgood is a spendthrift,   30
dissolute fellow.
HOARD
A very rascal.
MONEYLOVE
A midnight surfeiter.
HOARD
The spume of a brothel-house.
MONEYLOVE
True, sir! Which being well told in your worship's phrase,   35
may both heave him out of her mind, and drive a fair way for
me to the widow's affections.
HOARD
Attend me about five.

17–18 *be . . . countenance* seem favourable to
35 *phrase* manner of expression (*OED, s.v.,* 1. Cf. l. 47 below)

MONEYLOVE

With my best care, sir.   *Exit*

HOARD

Fool, thou hast left thy treasure with a thief,   40
To trust a widower with a suit in love!
Happy revenge, I hug thee! I have not only the means laid
before me, extremely to cross my adversary, and confound
the last hopes of his nephew, but thereby to enrich my state,
augment my revenues, and build mine own fortunes greater; 45
ha, ha!
I'll mar your phrase, o'erturn your flatteries,
Undo your windings, policies, and plots,
Fall like a secret and dispatchful plague
On your secured comforts. Why, I am able   50
To buy three of Lucre, thrice outbid him,
Let my out-monies be reckoned and all.

Enter three CREDITORS

1 CREDITOR

I am glad of this news.

2 CREDITOR

So are we, by my faith.

3 CREDITOR

Young Witgood will be a gallant again now.   55

HOARD

[*Listening*] Peace!

1 CREDITOR

I promise you, Master Cockpit, she's a mighty rich widow.

2 CREDITOR

Why, have you ever heard of her?

1 CREDITOR

Who? Widow Medler? she lies open to much rumour.

40–1 ed. prose in Qq
47 *phrase* gush of words in praise or flattery (*OED, s.v.*, 4)
49–52 ed. prose in Qq
49 *dispatchful* deadly
49 *plague* ed. plauge Q1
52 *out-monies* money lent out or invested and not immediately
   liquid

---

59 *open.* Another name for medlar, the fruit, was 'openarse'. See IV. v,
   142. The name is also appropriate for a prostitute because the fruit is
   not ready to eat until it is almost rotten (cf. *As You Like It*, III. ii,
   124–9).

3 CREDITOR

Four hundred a year, they say, in very good land.   60

1 CREDITOR

Nay, take't of my word, if you believe that, you believe the
least.

2 CREDITOR

And to see how close he keeps it!

1 CREDITOR

Oh, sir, there's policy in that, to prevent better suitors.

3 CREDITOR

He owes me a hundred pound, and I protest I never looked   65
for a penny.

1 CREDITOR

He little dreams of our coming; he'll wonder to see his
creditors upon him.   *Exeunt*

HOARD

Good, his creditors; I'll follow. This makes for me:
All know the widow's wealth; and 'tis well known   70
I can estate her fairly, ay, and will.
In this one chance shines a twice happy fate:
I both deject my foe, and raise my state. *Music*   *Exit*

[Act III, Scene i]

[Enter] WITGOOD *with his* CREDITORS

WITGOOD

Why, alas, my creditors, could you find no other time to
undo me but now? Rather your malice appears in this than
the justness of the debt.

1 CREDITOR

Master Witgood, I have forborne my money long.

WITGOOD

I pray, speak low, sir; what do you mean?   5

2 CREDITOR

We hear you are to be married suddenly to a rich country
widow.

WITGOOD

What can be kept so close but you creditors hear on't? Well,
'tis a lamentable state, that our chiefest afflicters should

63 *close* secret
69–71 ed. prose in Qq
69 *makes . . . me* works in my favour
73 *state* estate
s.d. ed. *Incipit ACT.* 3. Qq

first hear of our fortunes. Why, this is no good course, i'faith,   10
sirs; if ever you have hope to be satisfied, why do you seek
to confound the means that should work it? There's neither
piety, no, nor policy in that. Shine favourably now, why, I
may rise and spread again, to your great comforts.

1 CREDITOR
He says true, i'faith.   15

WITGOOD
Remove me now, and I consume for ever.

2 CREDITOR
Sweet gentleman!

WITGOOD
How can it thrive which from the sun you sever?

3 CREDITOR
It cannot, indeed!

WITGOOD
Oh, then, show patience! I shall have enough   20
To satisfy you all.

1 CREDITOR   Ay, if we could
Be content, a shame take us.

WITGOOD   For, look you,
I am but newly sure yet to the widow,
And what a rend might this discredit make!
Within these three days will I bind you lands   25
For your securities.

1 CREDITOR   No, good Master Witgood,
Would 'twere as much as we dare trust you with!

WITGOOD
I know you have been kind; however, now,
Either by wrong report, or false incitement,
Your gentleness is injured. In such   30
A state as this a man cannot want foes.
If on the sudden he begin to rise,
No man that lives can count his enemies.
You had some intelligence, I warrant ye,
From an ill-willer.   35

2 CREDITOR
Faith, we heard you brought up a rich widow, sir, and were
suddenly to marry her.

13 *piety* early form of *pity*
20–6 ed. prose in Qq
23 *sure* betrothed
28–31 ed. prose in Qq
34–5 ed. prose in Qq

WITGOOD

Ay, why there it was, I knew 'twas so: but since you are so
well resolved of my faith toward you, let me be so much
favoured of you, I beseech you all—   40

ALL

Oh, it shall not need, i'faith, sir—

WITGOOD

As to lie still awhile, and bury my debts in silence, till I be
fully possessed of the widow; for the truth is—I may tell you
as my friends—

ALL

Oh, oh, oh—   45

WITGOOD

I am to raise a little money in the city, toward the setting
forth of myself, for mine own credit, and your comfort. Now,
if my former debts should be divulged, all hope of my
proceedings were quite extinguished!

1 CREDITOR

[*Aside to* WITGOOD] Do you hear, sir? I may deserve your   50
custom hereafter; pray let my money be accepted before a
stranger's. Here's forty pound I received as I came to you;
if that may stand you in any stead, make use on't—nay, pray
sir, 'tis at your service.

WITGOOD

[*Aside*] You do so ravish me with kindness that   55
I'm constrained to play the maid, and take it!

1 CREDITOR

[*Aside*] Let none of them see it, I beseech you.

WITGOOD

[*Aside*] Fah!

1 CREDITOR

[*Aside*] I hope I shall be first in your remembrance
After the marriage rites.

WITGOOD   [*Aside*] Believe it firmly.   60

1 CREDITOR

So.—What, do you walk, sirs?

2 CREDITOR

I go.—[*Aside to* WITGOOD] Take no care, sir, for money to
furnish you; within this hour I'll send you sufficient.—
Come, Master Cockpit, we both stay for you.

39 *resolved* convinced
55–6 ed. prose in Qq
56 *play . . . it* say no—and acquiesce (proverbial)
59–60 ed. prose in Qq

3 CREDITOR

    I ha' lost a ring i'faith, I'll follow you presently [*Exeunt* 1   65
and 2 CREDITORS]—but you shall find it, sir; I know your
youth and expenses have disfurnished you of all jewels;
there's a ruby of twenty pound price, sir; bestow it upon
your widow.—What, man, 'twill call up her blood to you;
beside, if I might so much work with you, I would not have   70
you beholding to those blood-suckers for any money.

WITGOOD

    Not I, believe it.

3 CREDITOR

    They're a brace of cut-throats!

WITGOOD

    I know 'em.

3 CREDITOR

    Send a note of all your wants to my shop, and I'll supply you   75
instantly.

WITGOOD

    Say you so? Why, here's my hand then, no man living shall
do't but thyself.

3 CREDITOR

    Shall I carry it away from 'em both then?

WITGOOD

    I'faith, shalt thou!   80

3 CREDITOR

    Troth, then I thank you, sir.

WITGOOD

    Welcome good Master Cockpit!   *Exit* [3 CREDITOR]
Ha, ha, ha! why, is not this better now, than lying a-bed? I
perceive there's nothing conjures up wit sooner than poverty,
and nothing lays it down sooner than wealth and lechery!   85
This has some savour, yet oh! that I had the mortgage from
mine uncle as sure in possession as these trifles! I would
forswear brothel at noon day, and muscadine and eggs at
midnight.

Enter COURTESAN

COURTESAN

    Master Witgood? where are you?   90

WITGOOD

    Holla!

69 *blood* sexual appetite
79 *carry . . . away* win the day
88 *muscadine* a rich wine, taken with eggs as an aphrodisiac

COURTESAN
Rich news!

WITGOOD
Would 'twere all in plate.

COURTESAN
There's some in chains and jewels. I am so haunted with
suitors, Master Witgood, I know not which to dispatch first.   95

WITGOOD
You have the better term, by my faith.

COURTESAN
Among the number,
One Master Hoard, an ancient gentleman.

WITGOOD
Upon my life, my uncle's adversary.

COURTESAN
It may well hold so, for he rails on you,   100
Speaks shamefully of him.

WITGOOD   As I could wish it.

COURTESAN
I first denied him, but so cunningly,
It rather promised him assured hopes,
Than any loss of labour.

WITGOOD   Excellent.

COURTESAN
I expect him every hour, with gentlemen,   105
With whom he labours to make good his words,
To approve you riotous, your state consumed,
Your uncle—

WITGOOD
Wench, make up thy own fortunes now, do thyself a good
turn once in thy days. He's rich in money, moveables, and   110
lands; marry him, he's an old doting fool, and that's worth
all; marry him, 'twould be a great comfort to me to see thee
do well, i'faith; marry him, 'twould ease my conscience
well to see thee well bestowed; I have a care of thee, i'faith.

97–8 ed. prose in Qq   107–8 ed. prose in Qq
107 *approve* prove
110 *moveables* personal property

---

96 *term.* Witgood is playing with the two senses of *suitor*. During the
court sessions, when London was full of litigants, not only the lawyers
but also the prostitutes did very well for themselves. Cf. Dekker's and
Webster's *Westward Ho!*, 1604, III. iii, 13–14: 'there were many
Punkes in the Towne (as you know our Tearme is their Tearme)'.

COURTESAN

Thanks, sweet Master Witgood.   115

WITGOOD

I reach at farder happiness: first, I am sure it can be no harm
to thee, and there may happen goodness to me by it. Prose-
cute it well: let's send up for our wits, now we require their
best and most pregnant assistance!

COURTESAN

Step in, I think I hear 'em.   *Exit* [*with* WITGOOD]   120

Enter HOARD *and* GENTLEMEN *with the* HOST
[*as*] *serving-man*

HOARD

Art thou the widow's man? By my faith, sh'as a company of
proper men then.

HOST

I am the worst of six, sir; good enough for blue-coats.

HOARD

Hark hither: I hear say thou art in most credit with her.

HOST

Not so, sir.   125

HOARD

Come, come, thou'rt modest. There's a brace of royals;
prithee, help me to th' speech of her.

HOST

I'll do what I may, sir, always saving myself harmless.

HOARD

Go to, do't, I say; thou shalt hear better from me.

HOST

[*Aside*] Is not this a better place than five mark a year   130
standing wages? Say a man had but three such clients in a

116 *farder* farther
118 *our* ed. out Q1
123 *blue-coats* see II. i, 147
126 *royals* gold pieces worth about fifteen shillings
130 *mark* Middleton is using a term familiar to his audience as
    equivalent in England to 13s. 4d., though there was no actual coin
    of this amount
131 *standing* fixed

120 s.d. GENTLEMEN. Dyce suggests that these are Lamprey and Spitchcock,
    but see IV. i, where they are distinguished from numbered 'Gentlemen'.
    However, Middleton was careless about naming and counting his lesser
    characters (see III. iii, first s.d.), and the practical, theatrical point of
    view would support Dyce's suggestion.

day, methinks he might make a poor living on't; beside, I was
never brought up with so little honesty to refuse any man's
money; never. What gulls there are a' this side the world!
Now know I the widow's mind, none but my young master   135
comes in her clutches. Ha, ha, ha!   *Exit*

HOARD
  Now, my dear gentlemen, stand firmly to me;
  You know his follies, and my worth.
1 GENTLEMAN   We do, sir.
2 GENTLEMAN
  But, Master Hoard, are you sure he is not i'th' house now?
HOARD
  Upon my honesty I chose this time   140
  A' purpose, fit; the spendthrift is abroad.
  Assist me; here she comes.

                [Enter COURTESAN]
                     Now, my sweet widow.
COURTESAN
  Y'are welcome, Master Hoard.
HOARD
  Dispatch, sweet gentlemen, dispatch.—
  I am come, widow, to prove those my words   145
  Neither of envy sprung nor of false tongues,
  But such as their deserts and actions
  Do merit and bring forth, all which these gentlemen,
  Well known and better reputed, will confess.
COURTESAN
  I cannot tell   150
  How my affections may dispose of me,
  But surely if they find him so desertless,
  They'll have that reason to withdraw themselves.
  And therefore, gentlemen, I do entreat you,
  As you are fair in reputation,   155
  And in appearing form, so shine in truth.
  I am a widow, and, alas, you know,
  Soon overthrown; 'tis a very small thing
  That we withstand, our weakness is so great.

134 *gulls* dupes
137–8 ed. prose in Qq
146 *envy* malice
147 *their* i.e., Witgood's and Lucre's
148–9 ed. prose in Qq

Be partial unto neither, but deliver,   160
Without affection, your opinion.
HOARD
And that will drive it home.
COURTESAN
Nay, I beseech your silence, Master Hoard;
You are a party.
HOARD   Widow, not a word!
1 GENTLEMAN
The better first to work you to belief,   165
Know neither of us owe him flattery,
Nor t'other malice, but unbribed censure,
So help us our best fortunes.
COURTESAN   It suffices.
1 GENTLEMAN
That Witgood is a riotous, undone man,
Imperfect both in fame and in estate,   170
His debts wealthier than he, and executions
In wait for his due body, we'll maintain
With our best credit and our dearest blood.
COURTESAN
Nor land nor living, say you? Pray, take heed
You do not wrong the gentleman!
1 GENTLEMAN   What we speak   175
Our lives and means are ready to make good.
COURTESAN
Alas, how soon are we poor souls beguiled!
2 GENTLEMAN
And for his uncle—
HOARD   Let that come to me.
His uncle, a severe extortioner;
A tyrant at a forfeiture; greedy of others'   180
Miseries; one that would undo his brother,
Nay, swallow up his father, if he can,
Within the fathoms of his conscience.

161 *affection* prejudice
167 *t'other* i.e., Witgood (the *him* of the previous line refers to Hoard)
167 *censure* judgement
171 *executions* seizure of the goods or person of a debtor in default of
    payment
174–5 ed. prose in Qq
180–2 lineation ed.

183 *fathoms.* See I. i, 7–11 and note.

1 GENTLEMAN

    Nay, believe it, widow,

    You had not only matched yourself to wants,   185

    But in an evil and unnatural stock.

HOARD

    [*Aside*] Follow hard, gentlemen, follow hard!

COURTESAN

    Is my love so deceived? Before you all

    I do renounce him; on my knees I vow

    He ne'er shall marry me.   190

WITGOOD

    [*Looking in*] Heaven knows he never meant it!

HOARD

    [*Aside to* GENTLEMEN] There, take her at the bound.

1 GENTLEMAN

    Then with a new and pure affection,

    Behold yon gentleman, grave, kind, and rich,

    A match worthy yourself; esteeming him,   195

    You do regard your state.

HOARD

    [*Aside to* GENTLEMEN] I'll make her a jointure, say.

1 GENTLEMAN

    He can join land to land, and will possess you

    Of what you can desire.

2 GENTLEMAN   Come, widow, come.

COURTESAN

    The world is so deceitful!

1 GENTLEMAN   There 'tis deceitful,   200

    Where flattery, want, and imperfection lies;

    But none of these in him; push!

COURTESAN   Pray, sir—

1 GENTLEMAN

    Come, you widows are ever most backward when you should

    do yourselves most good; but were it to marry a chin not

    worth a hair now, then you would be forward enough! Come,   205

    clap hands, a match.

HOARD

    With all my heart, widow.—Thanks, gentlemen.

    I will deserve your labour, and thy love.

COURTESAN

    Alas, you love not widows but for wealth!

    I promise you I ha' nothing, sir.

192 *at the bound* at the first opportunity   198–9 ed. prose in Qq
204–5 *chin . . . hair* an impecunious youngster

HOARD   Well said, widow,   210
  Well said; thy love is all I seek, before
  These gentlemen.
COURTESAN   Now I must hope the best.
HOARD
  My joys are such they want to be expressed.
COURTESAN
  But, Master Hoard, one thing I must remember you of,
  before these gentlemen, your friends: how shall I suddenly   215
  avoid the loathed soliciting of that perjured Witgood, and his
  tedious, dissembling uncle, who this very day hath appointed
  a meeting for the same purpose too, where, had not truth
  come forth, I had been undone, utterly undone.
HOARD
  What think you of that, gentlemen?   220
1 GENTLEMAN
  'Twas well devised.
HOARD
  Hark thee, widow: train out young Witgood single; hasten
  him thither with thee, somewhat before the hour, where, at
  the place appointed, these gentlemen and myself will wait
  the opportunity, when, by some sleight removing him from   225
  thee, we'll suddenly enter and surprise thee, carry thee
  away by boat to Cole Harbour, have a priest ready, and
  there clap it up instantly. How lik'st it, widow?
COURTESAN
  In that it pleaseth you, it likes me well.
HOARD
  I'll kiss thee for those words.—Come, gentlemen;   230
  Still must I live a suitor to your favours,
  Still to your aid beholding.
1 GENTLEMAN   We're engaged, sir;
  'Tis for our credits now to see't well ended.
HOARD
  'Tis for your honours, gentlemen; nay, look to't;
  Not only in joy, but I in wealth excel.—   235
  No more sweet widow, but sweet wife, farewell.
COURTESAN
  Farewell, sir.   *Exeunt* [HOARD *and* GENTLEMEN]

210–12 ed. prose in Qq
215 *suddenly* shortly
217 *very* ed. very uery Q1
222 *train out* entice, decoy
229 *likes* is pleasing to

Enter WITGOOD

WITGOOD

Oh, for more scope! I could laugh eternally! Give you joy,
Mistress Hoard; I promise your fortune was good, forsooth;
y'ave fell upon wealth enough, and there's young gentlemen   240
enow can help you to the rest. Now it requires our wits; carry
thyself but heedfully now, and we are both—

[*Enter* HOST]

HOST

Master Witgood, your uncle.

WITGOOD

[*Aside to* COURTESAN] Cuds me! remove thyself a while; I'll
serve for him.   [*Exeunt* COURTESAN *and* HOST]   245

Enter LUCRE

LUCRE

Nephew, good morrow, nephew.

WITGOOD

The same to you, kind uncle.

LUCRE

How fares the widow? Does the meeting hold?

WITGOOD

Oh, no question of that, sir.

LUCRE

I'll strike the stroke, then, for thee; no more days.   250

WITGOOD

The sooner the better, uncle. Oh, she's mightily followed!

LUCRE

And yet so little rumoured!

WITGOOD

Mightily! Here comes one old gentleman, and he'll make her
a jointure of three hundred a year, forsooth; another wealthy
suitor will estate his son in his lifetime, and make him weigh   255
down the widow; here a merchant's son will possess her with
no less than three goodly lordships at once, which were all
pawns to his father.

LUCRE

Peace, nephew, let me hear no more of 'em; it mads me. Thou
shalt prevent 'em all. No words to the widow of my coming   260

245 *Entre* LUCRE ed. after l. 243 Qq
250 *days* postponements, days of grace (usurers' language. See IV. v,
77)
257 *lordships* estates   260 *prevent* get ahead of, anticipate

hither. Let me see—'tis now upon nine; before twelve,
nephew, we will have the bargain struck, we will, i'faith, boy.
WITGOOD
Oh, my precious uncle!   *Exit* [*with* LUCRE]

[Act III, Scene ii]

[*Enter*] HOARD *and his* NIECE

HOARD
Niece, sweet niece, prithee, have a care to my house; I leave
all to thy discretion. Be content to dream awhile; I'll have a
husband for thee shortly; put that care upon me, wench, for
in choosing wives and husbands I am only fortunate; I have
that gift given me.   *Exit*   5
NIECE
But 'tis not likely you should choose for me,
Since nephew to your chiefest enemy
Is he whom I affect; but, oh, forgetful!
Why dost thou flatter thy affections so,
With name of him that for a widow's bed   10
Neglects thy purer love? Can it be so,
Or does report dissemble?

[*Enter* GEORGE]

How now, sir?

GEORGE
A letter, with which came a private charge.
NIECE
Therein I thank your care. [*Exit* GEORGE] I know this hand:
Reads 'Dearer than sight, what the world reports of me,   15
yet believe not; rumour will alter shortly. Be thou constant;
I am still the same that I was in love, and I hope to be the
same in fortunes.
          Theodorus Witgood.'
I am resolved; no more shall fear or doubt   20
Raise their pale powers to keep affection out.   *Exit*

---

8 *affect* love   11 *it* ed. in Q1
20 *resolved* convinced

---

262 *i'faith.* Other editors print *faith*, probably because the initial *i* of Q1's
ifaith is badly damaged.

[Act III, Scene iii]

Enter, with a DRAWER, HOARD *and two* GENTLEMEN

DRAWER
You're very welcome, gentlemen.—Dick, show those
gentlemen the Pomegranate, there.

HOARD
Hist!

DRAWER
Up those stairs, gentlemen.

HOARD
Pist! drawer—   5

DRAWER
Anon, sir.

HOARD
Prithee, ask at the bar if a gentlewoman came not in lately.

DRAWER
William, at the bar, did you see any gentlewoman come in
lately? Speak you ay, speak you no?

[WILLIAM] *Within*
No, none came in yet but Mistress Florence.   10

DRAWER
He says none came in yet, sir, but one Mistress Florence.

HOARD
What is that Florence? a widow?

DRAWER
Yes, a Dutch widow.

HOARD
How?

DRAWER
That's an English drab, sir; give your worship good   15
morrow.   [*Exit*]

---

2 *Pomegranate* tavern rooms were named thus instead of numbered

---

s.d. *two* GENTLEMEN. Note Q1's assignment of speech, l. 30. Spencer's theory
that this *two* 'indicates reduction of personnel in the interest of economy'
is untenable, since it suggests a playhouse provenance for the MS of Q1,
to which all the evidence runs counter. In light of the fact that the first
gentleman seems to 'join their hands' at III. i, 206, it is best to explain
the anomaly as being due to authorial carelessness about minor characters. See III. i, 120, IV. v, 5, and V. ii, 19 and 41. As at III. i, 120 the
'two Gentlemen' are probably Lamprey and Spitchcock.

1 *Dick*. Off-stage, like William at l. 10.

HOARD
    A merry knave, i'faith! I shall remember a Dutch widow the
    longest day of my life.

1 GENTLEMAN
    Did not I use most art to win the widow?

2 GENTLEMAN
    You shall pardon me for that, sir; Master Hoard knows I took   20
    her at best vantage.

HOARD
    What's that, sweet gentlemen, what's that?

2 GENTLEMAN
    He will needs bear me down that his art only wrought with
    the widow most.

HOARD
    Oh, you did both well, gentlemen, you did both well, I   25
    thank you.

1 GENTLEMAN
    I was the first that moved her.

HOARD   You were, i'faith.

2 GENTLEMAN
    But it was I that took her at the bound.

HOARD
    Ay, that was you; faith, gentlemen, 'tis right.

1 GENTLEMAN
    I boasted least, but 'twas I joined their hands.   30

HOARD
    By th' mass, I think he did. You did all well,
    Gentlemen, you did all well; contend no more.

1 GENTLEMAN
    Come, yon room's fittest.

HOARD   True, 'tis next the door.
                    Exit [*with* GENTLEMEN]

       Enter WITGOOD, COURTESAN, [DRAWER] *and* HOST

DRAWER
    You're very welcome; please you to walk up stairs, cloth's
    laid, sir.   35

COURTESAN
    Upstairs? troth, I am weary, Master Witgood.

WITGOOD
    Rest yourself here awhile, widow; we'll have a cup of musca-
    dine in this little room.

30 1 GENTLEMAN ed. 3. Qq
31–2 ed. prose in Qq   37 *muscadine* see III. i, 88

DRAWER

A cup of muscadine? You shall have the best, sir.

WITGOOD

But, do you hear, sirrah?   40

DRAWER

Do you call? Anon, sir.

WITGOOD

What is there provided for dinner?

DRAWER

I cannot readily tell you, sir; if you please, you may go into
the kitchen and see yourself, sir; many gentlemen of worship
do use to do it, I assure you, sir.   [*Exit*]   45

HOST

A pretty familiar prigging rascal, he has his part without
book!

WITGOOD

Against you are ready to drink to me, widow, I'll be present
to pledge you.

COURTESAN

Nay, I commend your care, 'tis done well of you.   50

                                      [*Exit* WITGOOD]

'Las, what have I forgot!

HOST

What, Mistress?

COURTESAN

I slipped my wedding ring off when I washed, and left it at my
lodging; prithee run, I shall be sad without it.   [*Exit* HOST]
So, he's gone!—Boy!   55

                     [*Enter* BOY]

BOY

Anon, forsooth.

COURTESAN

Come hither, sirrah: learn secretly if one Master Hoard, an
ancient gentleman, be about house.

BOY

I heard such a one named.

COURTESAN

Commend me to him.   60

           Enter HOARD *with* GENTLEMEN

46 *prigging* haggling or suave. The cant word need not be taken in
   any strictly literal sense
46–7 *without book* off by heart   48 *Against* before
51 *'Las* ed. asse Qq. A letter has obviously dropped out in Q1

HOARD
   I'll do thy commendations!
COURTESAN
   Oh, you come well: away, to boat, begone.
HOARD
   Thus wise men are revenged, give two for one.   *Exeunt*

                  Enter WITGOOD *and* VINTNER

WITGOOD
   I must request
   You, sir, to show extraordinary care;   65
   My uncle comes with gentlemen, his friends,
   And 'tis upon a making.
VINTNER   Is it so?
   I'll give a special charge, good Master Witgood.
   May I be bold to see her?
WITGOOD   Who, the widow?
   With all my heart, i'faith, I'll bring you to her!   70
VINTNER
   If she be a Staffordshire gentlewoman, 'tis much if I know
   her not.
WITGOOD
   How now? boy, drawer!
VINTNER
   Hie!
                       [*Enter* BOY]
BOY
   Do you call, sir?   75
WITGOOD
   Went the gentlewoman up that was here?
BOY
   Up, sir? she went out, sir.
WITGOOD
   Out, sir?
BOY
   Out, sir: one Master Hoard with a guard of gentlemen carried
   her out at back door, a pretty while since, sir.   80
WITGOOD
   Hoard? death and darkness, Hoard?

64–7 ed. prose in Qq
67 *upon a making* concerning a matchmaking
68–9 ed. prose in Qq   69 *the* ed. he Qq

---

61 *I'll.* Eleven of the extant copies of Q1 read 'I bee' (which modern
   editors emend to 'Ay, boy'); only three have the correct 'Ile'.

Enter HOST

HOST
  The devil of ring I can find!
WITGOOD
  How now, what news? where's the widow?
HOST
  My mistress? is she not here, sir?
WITGOOD
  More madness yet.
HOST   She sent me for a ring.   85
WITGOOD
  A plot, a plot! To boat! she's stole away!
HOST
  What?

Enter LUCRE *with* GENTLEMEN

WITGOOD
  Follow, enquire old Hoard, my uncle's adversary—
                                        [*Exit* HOST]
LUCRE
  Nephew, what's that?
WITGOOD   Thrice miserable wretch!
LUCRE
  Why, what's the matter?
VINTNER   The widow's borne away, sir.   90
LUCRE
  Ha? passion of me!—A heavy welcome, gentlemen.
1 GENTLEMAN
  The widow gone?
LUCRE   Who durst attempt it?
WITGOOD
  Who but old Hoard, my uncle's adversary?
LUCRE
  How!
WITGOOD
  With his confederates.   95
LUCRE
  Hoard, my deadly enemy! Gentlemen, stand to me,
  I will not bear it, 'tis in hate of me;
  That villain seeks my shame, nay thirsts my blood;
  He owes me mortal malice.
  I'll spend my wealth on this despiteful plot,   100
  Ere he shall cross me and my nephew thus.

98–9 ed. prose in Qq
98 *thirsts* ed. thrifts Qq

WITGOOD
  So maliciously.

                    Enter HOST

LUCRE
  How now, you treacherous rascal?
HOST
  That's none of my name, sir.
WITGOOD
  Poor soul, he knew not on't.   105
LUCRE
  I'm sorry. I see then 'twas a mere plot.
HOST
  I traced 'em nearly—
LUCRE   Well?
HOST   And hear for certain
  They have took Cole Harbour.
LUCRE   The devil's sanctuary!
  They shall not rest, I'll pluck her from his arms.
  Kind and dear gentlemen,   110
  If ever I had seat within your breasts—
1 GENTLEMAN
  No more, good sir, it is a wrong to us,
  To see you injured; in a cause so just
  We'll spend our lives, but we will right our friends.
LUCRE
  Honest and kind! come, we have delayed too long: 115
  Nephew, take comfort; a just cause is strong.
WITGOOD
  That's all my comfort, uncle.
          Exeunt [LUCRE, GENTLEMEN, VINTNER *and* BOY]
                    Ha, ha, ha!
  Now may events fall luckily, and well:
  He that ne'er strives, says wit, shall ne'er excel.   *Exit*

---

107 *nearly* closely
107–8 lineation ed.
110–11 lineation ed.   117 s.d. ed. after l. 116 Qq
119 *wit*, ed. wit Qq (Wit is personified again at IV. iii, 52)

---

108 *Cole Harbour.* See II. i, 237, and the ironic contrast in Lucre's view of
   the place.

[Act III, Scene iv]

Enter DAMPIT, *the Usurer, drunk*

DAMPIT

When did I say my prayers? In anno '88, when the great
armada was coming; and in anno '99, when the great
thundering and lightning was, I prayed heartily then, i'faith,
to overthrow Poovies' new buildings; I kneeled by my
great iron chest, I remember.   5

[*Enter* AUDREY]

AUDREY

Master Dampit, one may hear you, before they see you; you
keep sweet hours, Master Dampit; we were all abed three
hours ago.

DAMPIT

Audrey?

AUDREY

Oh, y'are a fine gentleman.   10

DAMPIT

So I am, i'faith, and a fine scholar. Do you use to go to bed so
early, Audrey?

AUDREY

Call you this early, Master Dampit?

DAMPIT

Why, is't not one of clock i'th' morning? Is not that early
enough? Fetch me a glass of fresh beer.   15

3 *lightning* ed. Lighting Q1   11 *bed* ed. bed Bed Q1

---

s.d. *Usurer.* Presumably Dampit turned to usury after his 'trampling' days
were done. He continues to be spoken of as both petty lawyer and
usurer throughout the play (see especially IV. v, 12, 54, 151).

2 *'99.* Most modern editors emend either to *'89* or to *'98*, when John
Stow's *Survey of London*, 1603, records tremendous storms (none such
is recorded for '99). Emendation is unnecessary: as Spencer says, 'the
point is the long lapse of time' between Dampit's praying fits, and there
is no reason to suppose that Middleton aspired to meteorological accuracy.

4 *Poovies'.* Sampson notes tentatively that a certain Povey erected a
timber building in Paul's Churchyard, after James I, in 1605 and 1607,
had ordered no more houses in the city to be built of wood. It had to be
pulled down. This identification is not conclusive, however. E. H.
Sugden, *A Topographical Dictionary to the Works of Shakespeare and
His Fellow Dramatists*, 1925, p. 418, says that possibly Powis House, at
one corner of Lincoln's Inn Fields, is meant, but Spencer may be right
when he suggests that the name 'may be taken at random and intended
merely to illustrate Dampit's malevolence'.

AUDREY
Here, I have warmed your nightcap for you, Master Dampit.
DAMPIT
Draw it on then.—I am very weak, truly; I have not eaten
so much as the bulk of an egg these three days.
AUDREY
You have drunk the more, Master Dampit.
DAMPIT
What's that?   20
AUDREY
You mought, an you would, Master Dampit.
DAMPIT
I answer you I cannot. Hold your prating; you prate too
much and understand too little. Are you answered? Give
me a glass of beer.
AUDREY
May I ask you how you do, Master Dampit?   25
DAMPIT
How do I? I'faith, naught.
AUDREY
I never knew you do otherwise.
DAMPIT
I eat not one penn'ort' of bread these two years. Give me a
glass of fresh beer—I am not sick, nor I am not well.
AUDREY
Take this warm napkin about your neck, sir, whilst I help to   30
make you unready.
DAMPIT
How now, Audrey-prater, with your scurvy devices, what
say you now?
AUDREY
What say I, Master Dampit? I say nothing but that you are
very weak.   35
DAMPIT
Faith, thou hast more coney-catching devices than all
London!

21 *mought* obsolete form of *might*
31 *make . . . unready* undress you
36 *coney-catching devices* cheating stratagems

---

28 *not one penn'ort' of bread.* Dampit has some of Falstaff's characteristics:
cf. Falstaff's 'one halfpennyworth of bread to this intolerable deal of
sack.' (1 *Henry IV*, II. iv, 598–9).

AUDREY
Why, Master Dampit, I never deceived you in all my life!
DAMPIT
Why was that? Because I never did trust thee.
AUDREY
I care not what you say, Master Dampit!   40
DAMPIT
Hold thy prating. I answer thee, thou art a beggar, a quean,
and a bawd; are you answered?
AUDREY
Fie, Master Dampit! a gentleman, and have such words?
DAMPIT
Why, thou base drudge of infortunity, thou kitchen-stuff
drab of beggary, roguery and coxcombry, thou cavernesed   45
quean of foolery, knavery and bawdreaminy, I'll tell thee
what, I will not give a louse for thy fortunes.
AUDREY
No, Master Dampit? And there's a gentleman comes a-
wooing to me, and he doubts nothing but that you will get me
from him.   50
DAMPIT
I? If I would either have thee or lie with thee for two
thousand pound, would I might be damned! Why, thou base,
impudent quean of foolery, flattery and coxcombry, are you
answered?
AUDREY
Come, will you rise and go to bed, sir?   55
DAMPIT
Rise, and go to bed too, Audrey? How does Mistress Proser-
pine?
AUDREY
Fooh—

41 *quean* strumpet
44 *infortunity* misfortune
44 *kitchen-stuff* refuse, slops
45 *cavernesed* cavernous? (i.e., she is like a cavern full of foolery)
46 *bawdreaminy* bawdry
49 *doubts* fears
56 *Mistress* ed. Misters Q1

56–7 *Mistress Proserpine.* Probably Dampit's surrealistically drunken
name for a bawd or prostitute 'in the liberties'. He could mean Audrey
herself, implying that she is a witch (Proserpine was sometimes identified with Hecate). Middleton intended Dampit to be incoherent.

DAMPIT
  She's as fine a philosopher of a stinkard's wife as any within
  the liberties—fah, fah, Audrey!   60
AUDREY
  How now, Master Dampit?
DAMPIT
  Fie upon't, what a choice of stinks is here! What hast thou
  done, Audrey? Fie upon't, here's a choice of stinks indeed!
  Give me a glass of fresh beer, and then I will to bed.
AUDREY
  It waits for you above, sir.   65
DAMPIT
  Foh! I think they burn horns in Barnard's Inn; if ever I
  smelt such an abominable stink, usury forsake me.   [*Exit*]
AUDREY
  They be the stinking nails of his trampling feet, and he
  talks of burning of horns.   *Exit*

[Act IV, Scene i]

Enter at Cole Harbour, HOARD, *the* WIDOW, [LAMPREY, SPITCH-
      COCK] *and* GENTLEMEN, *he married now*

1 GENTLEMAN
  Join hearts, join hands,
  In wedlock's bands,
  Never to part
  Till death cleave your heart;
  You shall forsake all other women;   5
  You lords, knights, gentlemen and yeomen.
  What my tongue slips,
  Make up with your lips.

60 *liberties* suburbs, in which the brothels flourished
62 *is here* ed. here is Qq
66 *horns* either ink-wells (made of horn) or the translucent horn used
      to protect leaves of paper in reading
68 *stinking . . . feet* see I. iv, 44
s.d.ed. *Incipit ACT.* 4.Qq
  1–4 lineation ed.
  7 *slips* neglects, overlooks
  7–8 lineation ed.

66 *Barnard's Inn.* An Inn of Chancery, on the south side of Holborn. The
    reference to the burning of horns is probably best understood as a wild
    flight of the drunkard's 'fantastical' imagination.

HOARD
 Give you joy, Mistress Hoard; let the kiss come about.
                                        [*Knocking*]
 Who knocks? Convey my little pig-eater out.   10
LUCRE [*within*]
 Hoard!
HOARD
 Upon my life, my adversary, gentlemen.
LUCRE [*within*]
 Hoard, open the door, or we will force it ope:
 Give us the widow.
HOARD   Gentlemen, keep 'em out.
LAMPREY
 He comes upon his death that enters here.   15
LUCRE [*within*]
 My friends assist me.
HOARD   He has assistants, gentlemen.
LAMPREY
 Tut, nor him, nor them, we in this action fear.
LUCRE [*within*]
 Shall I, in peace, speak one word with the widow?
COURTESAN
 Husband and gentlemen, hear me but a word.
HOARD
 Freely, sweet wife.
COURTESAN   Let him in peaceably;   20
 You know we're sure from any act of his.
HOARD
 Most true.
COURTESAN
 You may stand by and smile at his old weakness;
 Let me alone to answer him.
HOARD   Content,
 'Twill be good mirth, i'faith; how think you gentlemen?   25
LAMPREY
 Good gullery!
HOARD   Upon calm conditions let him in.

 9 *come about* circulate
10 *pig-eater* a term of endearment
20–1 ed. prose in Qq
23–4 ed. prose in Qq
23 COURTESAN ed *Lu.* Qq
24 *let . . . alone* leave it to me
26 *gullery* trickery

LUCRE [*within*]
  All spite and malice—
LAMPREY   Hear me, Master Lucre:
  So you will vow a peaceful entrance
  With those your friends, and only exercise
  Calm conference with the widow, without fury,   30
  The passage shall receive you.
LUCRE [*within*]   I do vow it.
LAMPREY
  Then enter and talk freely, here she stands.

            Enter LUCRE, [GENTLEMEN, *and* HOST]
LUCRE
  Oh, Master Hoard, your spite has watched the hour;
  You're excellent at vengeance, Master Hoard.
HOARD
  Ha, ha, ha!
LUCRE   I am the fool you laugh at: 35
  You are wise, sir, and know the seasons well.
  Come hither, widow: why is it thus?
  Oh, you have done me infinite disgrace,
  And your own credit no small injury!
  Suffer mine enemy so despitefully   40
  To bear you from my nephew! oh, I had
  Rather half my substance had been forfeit,
  And begged by some starved rascal!
COURTESAN
  Why, what would you wish me do, sir?
  I must not overthrow my state for love: 45
  We have too many precedents for that;
  From thousands of our wealthy undone widows
  One may derive some wit. I do confess,
  I loved your nephew, nay, I did affect him,
  Against the mind and liking of my friends;   50
  Believed his promises, lay here in hope
  Of flattered living, and the boast of lands:
  Coming to touch his wealth and state indeed,

27–9 ed. prose in Qq
28 *entrance* trisyllabic
32 s.d. ed. after *receive you*, l. 31, in Qq
33–7 ed. prose in Qq
41–3 lineation ed.
49 *affect* love
50 *friends* ed. friend Q1
52 *flattered* too favourably represented

It appears dross; I find him not the man,
Imperfect, mean, scarce furnished of his needs;   55
In words, fair lordships, in performance, hovels:
Can any woman love the thing that is not?

LUCRE
Broke you for this?

COURTESAN   Was it not cause too much?
Send to enquire his state: most part of it
Lay two years mortgaged in his uncle's hands.   60

LUCRE
Why, say it did, you might have known my mind;
I could have soon restored it.

COURTESAN
Ay, had I but seen any such thing performed,
Why, 'twould have tied my affection, and contained
Me in my first desires: do you think, i'faith,   65
That I could twine such a dry oak as this,
Had promise in your nephew took effect?

LUCRE
Why, and there's no time past; and rather than
My adversary should thus thwart my hopes,
I would—   70

COURTESAN
Tut, y'ave been ever full of golden speech.
If words were lands, your nephew would be rich.

LUCRE
Widow, believe it, I vow by my best bliss,
Before these gentlemen, I will give in
The mortgage to my nephew instantly,   75
Before I sleep or eat.

1 GENTLEMAN   We'll pawn our credits,
Widow, what he speaks shall be performed
In fulness.

LUCRE   Nay, more: I will estate him
In farder blessings; he shall be my heir.
I have no son;   80
I'll bind myself to that condition.

COURTESAN
When I shall hear this done, I shall soon yield
To reasonable terms.

LUCRE   In the mean season,

56 *performance* fulfilment of promises
61–70 ed. prose in Qq
76–8 ed. prose in Qq   82–3 ed. prose in Qq

Will you protest, before these gentlemen,
To keep yourself as you are now at this present?   85

COURTESAN
I do protest before these gentlemen,
I will be as clear then, as I am now.

LUCRE
I do believe you. Here's your own honest servant,
I'll take him along with me.

COURTESAN   Ay, with all my heart.

LUCRE
He shall see all performed and bring you word.   90

COURTESAN
That's all I wait for.

HOARD
What, have you finished, Master Lucre? Ha, ha, ha, ha!

LUCRE
So laugh, Hoard, laugh at your poor enemy, do;
The wind may turn, you may be laughed at too.
Yes, marry, may you, sir.—Ha, ha, ha!   95

HOARD   *Exeunt* [LUCRE, GENTLEMEN *and* HOST]
Ha, ha, ha! If every man that swells in malice
Could be revenged as happily as I,
He would choose hate and forswear amity.
What did he say, wife, prithee?

COURTESAN
Faith, spoke to ease his mind.

HOARD   Oh—oh—oh!   100

COURTESAN
You know now little to any purpose.

HOARD
True, true, true.

COURTESAN   He would do mountains now.

HOARD
Ay, ay, ay, ay.

LAMPREY   Y'ave struck him dead, Master Hoard.

SPITCHCOCK
And his nephew desperate.

HOARD   I know't, sirs, I.
Never did man so crush his enemy!   *Exeunt* 105

87 *clear* pure   93–5 ed. prose in Qq
102 *do mountains* give the world (to regain the 'widow')
104 *And* ed. I and Q1

85 Lucre does not know that Hoard's marriage has already taken place.

[Act IV, Scene ii]

Enter LUCRE *with* GENTLEMEN [*and* HOST], *meeting* SAM FREEDOM

LUCRE
My son-in-law, Sam Freedom! Where's my nephew?

SAM
O man in lamentation, father!

LUCRE
How?

SAM
He thumps his breast like a gallant dicer that has lost his
doublet, and stands in's shirt to do penance.   5

LUCRE
Alas, poor gentleman.

SAM
I warrant you may hear him sigh in a still evening to your
house at Highgate.

LUCRE
I prithee, send him in.

SAM
Were it to do a greater matter, I will not stick with you, sir,   10
in regard you married my mother.   [*Exit*]

LUCRE
Sweet gentlemen, cheer him up; I will but fetch the mortgage, and return to you instantly.   *Exit*

1 GENTLEMAN
We'll do our best, sir.—See where he comes,
E'en joyless and regardless of all form.   15

[*Enter* WITGOOD]

2 GENTLEMAN
Why, how now, Master Witgood? Fie, you a firm scholar,
and an understanding gentleman, and give your best parts
to passion?

1 GENTLEMAN
Come, fie!

1 *son-in-law* stepson
1 ed. as two lines in Qq (my . . . lawe/*Sam* . . . Nephew?)
10 *stick . . . you* begrudge you
16 *how now* ed. how Q1   18 *passion* sorrow

2 *O man in lamentation.* There was an old tune 'O man in desperation',
mentioned in Nashe's *Summer's Last Will and Testament*, 1600, and
Peele's *The Old Wives' Tale*, 1590.

WITGOOD
    Oh, gentlemen—   20
1 GENTLEMAN
    Sorrow of me, what a sigh was there, sir!
    Nine such widows are not worth it.
WITGOOD
    To be borne from me by that lecher, Hoard!
1 GENTLEMAN
    That vengeance is your uncle's, being done
    More in despite to him, than wrong to you.   25
    But we bring comfort now.
WITGOOD   I beseech you, gentlemen—
2 GENTLEMAN
    Cheer thyself, man, there's hope of her, i'faith!
WITGOOD
    Too gladsome to be true.

Enter LUCRE

LUCRE   Nephew, what cheer?
    Alas, poor gentleman, how art thou changed!
    Call thy fresh blood into thy cheeks again: 30
    She comes—
WITGOOD   Nothing afflicts me so much
    But that it is your adversary, uncle,
    And merely plotted in despite of you.
LUCRE
    Ay, that's it mads me, spites me! I'll spend my wealth ere
    he shall carry her so, because I know 'tis only to spite me.   35
    Ay, this is it.—Here, nephew [*giving a paper*], before these
    kind gentlemen I deliver in your mortgage, my promise to
    the widow; see, 'tis done. Be wise, you're once more master
    of your own; the widow shall perceive now, you are not alto-
    gether such a beggar as the world reputes you: you can make   40
    shift to bring her to three hundred a year, sir.
1 GENTLEMAN
    Berlady, and that's no toy, sir.
LUCRE
    A word, nephew.
1 GENTLEMAN [*to* HOST]
    Now you may certify the widow.

28–31 ed. prose in Qq
33 *merely* simply, absolutely
35 *carry* win
42 *Berlady* By our Lady

LUCRE
You must conceive it aright, nephew, now; 45
To do you good I am content to do this.
WITGOOD
I know it, sir.
LUCRE
But your own conscience can tell I had it
Dearly enough of you.
WITGOOD   Ay, that's most certain.
LUCRE
Much money laid out, beside many a journey 50
To fetch the rent; I hope you'll think on't, nephew.
WITGOOD
I were worse than a beast else, i'faith.
LUCRE
Although to blind the widow and the world
I out of policy do't, yet there's a conscience, nephew.
WITGOOD
Heaven forbid else!
LUCRE   When you are full possessed, 55
'Tis nothing to return it.
WITGOOD
Alas, a thing quickly done, uncle.
LUCRE
Well said! you know I give it you but in trust.
WITGOOD
Pray let me understand you rightly, uncle:
You give it me but in trust? 60
LUCRE
No.
WITGOOD
That is, you trust me with it.
LUCRE
True, true.
WITGOOD
[*Aside*] But if ever I trust you with it again, would I might
be trussed up for my labour! 65
LUCRE
You can all witness, gentlemen, and you, sir yeoman?
HOST
My life for yours, sir, now I know my mistress's mind so

45–54 ed. prose in Qq
65 *trussed up* hanged
67 *so* ed. to Q1 too Q2

well toward your nephew; let things be in preparation and
I'll train her hither in most excellent fashion.   *Exit*

LUCRE

A good old boy—wife, Jinny!   70

Enter WIFE

WIFE

What's the news, sir?

LUCRE

The wedding day's at hand: prithee, sweet wife, express thy
housewifery; thou'rt a fine cook, I know't; thy first husband
married thee out of an alderman's kitchen; go to, he raised
thee for raising of paste. What! here's none but friends;   75
most of our beginnings must be winked at.—Gentlemen, I
invite you all to my nephew's wedding against Thursday
morning.

1 GENTLEMAN

With all our hearts, and we shall joy to see
Your enemy so mocked.

LUCRE   He laughed at me,   80
Gentlemen; ha, ha, ha!   *Exeunt* [*all but* WITGOOD]

WITGOOD   He has no conscience, faith,
Would laugh at them; they laugh at one another!
Who then can be so cruel? Troth, not I;
I rather pity now, than aught envy.
I do conceive such joy in mine own happiness,   85
I have no leisure yet to laugh at their follies.
[*To the mortgage*] Thou soul of my estate I kiss thee,
I miss life's comfort when I miss thee.
Oh, never will we part again,
Until I leave the sight of men.   90
We'll ne'er trust conscience of our kin,
Since cozenage brings that title in.   [*Exit*]

69 *train* entice
70 *Jinny* ed. Girnne Qq
79–82 ed. prose in Qq
84 *envy* bear malice
85–6 ed. prose in Qq
92 *Since . . . in* since cozenage (or cousinship) introduces that name
    (i.e., of *kin*). Another variant of the cousin-cozen pun

[Act IV, Scene iii]

Enter three CREDITORS

1 CREDITOR
I'll wait these seven hours but I'll see him caught.
2 CREDITOR
Faith, so will I.
3 CREDITOR
Hang him, prodigal, he's stripped of the widow.
1 CREDITOR
A' my troth, she's the wiser; she has made the happier choice; and I wonder of what stuff those widows' hearts are made of, that will marry unfledged boys before comely thrum-chinned gentlemen.

Enter a BOY

BOY
News, news, news!
1 CREDITOR
What, boy?
BOY
The rioter is caught.
1 CREDITOR
So, so, so, so! It warms me at the heart; I love a' life to see dogs upon men. Oh, here he comes.

Enter WITGOOD *with* SERGEANTS

WITGOOD
My last joy was so great it took away the sense of all future afflictions. What a day is here o'ercast! How soon a black tempest rises!
1 CREDITOR
Oh, we may speak with you now, sir! What's become of your rich widow? I think you may cast your cap at the widow, may you not, sir?
2 CREDITOR
He a rich widow? Who, a prodigal, a daily rioter, and a nightly vomiter? He a widow of account? He a hole i'th' Counter!
WITGOOD
You do well, my masters, to tyrannize over misery, to afflict

6 *thrum-chinned* bearded. The *thrum* was the waste end of the warp
20 *hole* one of the worst cells
21 *Counter* a city prison for debtors

the afflicted; 'tis a custom you have here amongst you; I
would wish you never leave it, and I hope you'll do as I bid
you.   25

1 CREDITOR
Come, come, sir, what say you extempore now to your bill
of a hundred pound? A sweet debt, for frotting your doub-
lets.

2 CREDITOR
Here's mine of forty.

3 CREDITOR
Here's mine of fifty.   30

WITGOOD
Pray, sirs—you'll give me breath?

1 CREDITOR
No sir, we'll keep you out of breath still; then we shall be sure
you will not run away from us.

WITGOOD
Will you but hear me speak?

2 CREDITOR
You shall pardon us for that, sir; we know you have too fair a   35
tongue of your own: you overcame us too lately, a shame take
you! We are like to lose all that for want of witnesses; we
dealt in policy then: always when we strive to be most politic
we prove most coxcombs; *non plus ultra*. I perceive by us
we're not ordained to thrive by wisdom, and therefore we   40
must be content to be tradesmen.

WITGOOD
Give me but reasonable time, and I protest I'll make you
ample satisfaction.

1 CREDITOR
Do you talk of reasonable time to us?

WITGOOD
'Tis true, beasts know no reasonable time.   45

2 CREDITOR
We must have either money or carcass.

WITGOOD
Alas, what good will my carcass do you?

---

27 *frotting* rubbing with perfume. Cf. Jonson's *Cynthia's Revels*,
V. iv, 312

---

39 *non plus ultra*. No farther. A reference to the *ne plus ultra* said to have
been inscribed on the Pillars of Hercules (Gibraltar and Mt. Abyla),
the traditional limit to navigation.

3 CREDITOR
Oh 'tis a secret delight we have amongst us! We that are used
to keep birds in cages, have the heart to keep men in prison,
I warrant you.   50

WITGOOD
[*Aside*] I perceive I must crave a little more aid from my
wits: do but make shift for me this once, and I'll forswear
ever to trouble you in the like fashion hereafter; I'll have
better employment for you, an I live.—You'll give me leave,
my masters, to make trial of my friends, and raise all means   55
I can?

1 CREDITOR
That's our desires, sir.

Enter HOST

HOST
Master Witgood.

WITGOOD
Oh, art thou come?

HOST
May I speak one word with you in private, sir?   60

WITGOOD
No, by my faith, canst thou; I am in hell here, and the devils
will not let me come to thee.

CREDITORS
Do you call us devils? You shall find us Puritans.—Bear him
away; let 'em talk as they go; we'll not stand to hear 'em.—
Ah, sir, am I a devil? I shall think the better of myself as   65
long as I live: a devil, i'faith!   *Exeunt*

Act IV, Scene iv

Enter HOARD

HOARD
What a sweet blessing hast thou, Master Hoard, above a
multitude! Wilt thou never be thankful? How dost thou think
to be blest another time? Or dost thou count this the full
measure of thy happiness? By my troth, I think thou dost:
not only a wife large in possessions, but spacious in content: 5
she's rich, she's young, she's fair, she's wise; when I wake, I
think of her lands—that revives me; when I go to bed, I dream

63 CREDITORS ed. *Cit.* (i.e., Citizens) Qq (mod. eds. erroneously
    emend to 1 CRED.)
6 *wise* ed. wife Q1

of her beauty—and that's enough for me; she's worth four
hundred a year in her very smock, if a man knew how to use it.
But the journey will be all, in troth, into the country; to ride to   10
her lands in state and order following my brother and other
worshipful gentlemen, whose companies I ha' sent down for
already, to ride along with us in their goodly decorum beards,
their broad velvet cassocks, and chains of gold twice or thrice
double; against which time I'll entertain some ten men of   15
mine own into liveries, all of occupations or qualities: I will
not keep an idle man about me; the sight of which will so
vex my adversary Lucre—for we'll pass by his door of
purpose, make a little stand for the nonce, and have our
horses curvet before the window—certainly he will never   20
endure it, but run up and hang himself presently!

[*Enter* SERVANT]

How now, sirrah, what news? Any that offer their service to
me yet?

SERVANT
Yes, sir, there are some i'th' hall that wait for your worship's
liking, and desire to be entertained.   25

HOARD
Are they of occupation?

SERVANT
They are men fit for your worship, sir.

HOARD
Say'st so? send 'em all in! [*Exit* SERVANT] To see ten men ride
after me in watchet liveries, with orange-tawny capes, 'twill
cut his comb, i'faith.   30

Enter ALL [*i.e.*, TAILOR, BARBER, PERFUMER, FALCONER,
and HUNTSMAN]

13 *decorum* noun used in its original adjectival function
14 *cassocks* long loose coats, often worn by usurers
15–16 *entertain . . . into liveries* employ as servants
19 *the* ed. omitted Qq
29 *watchet* sky blue
30 s.d. after l. 32 in Qq

---

21 *hang himself*. The traditional end for a usurer when overtaken by
despair. See C. T. Wright, 'Some Conventions Regarding the Usurer
in Elizabethan Literature', *SP*, XXXI (1934), 192–6.
29 *orange-tawny*. Cf. Bacon's *Of Usury*: '*Vsurers* should have Orange-
tawney Bonnets, because they doe *Judaize*' (E. Arber, ed., *A Harmony
of the Essays . . . of Francis Bacon*, 1895, p. 541).

How now? Of what occupation are you, sir?

TAILOR

A tailor, an't please your worship.

HOARD

A tailor? Oh, very good: you shall serve to make all the
liveries.—What are you, sir?

BARBER

A barber, sir.   35

HOARD

A barber? very needful: you shall shave all the house, and, if
need require, stand for a reaper i'th' summer time.—You,
sir?

PERFUMER

A perfumer.

HOARD

I smelt you before. Perfumers, of all men, had need carry   40
themselves uprightly, for if they were once knaves they would
be smelt out quickly.—To you, sir?

FALCONER

A falconer, an't please your worship.

HOARD

Sa ho, sa ho, sa ho!—And you, sir?

HUNTSMAN

A huntsman, sir.   45

HOARD

There, boy, there, boy, there, boy! I am not so old but I have
pleasant days to come. I promise you, my masters, I take
such a good liking to you, that I entertain you all; I put you
already into my countenance, and you shall be shortly in my
livery; but especially you two, my jolly falconer and my   50
bonny huntsman, we shall have most need of you at my
wife's manor houses i'th' country; there's goodly parks and
champion grounds for you; we shall have all our sports within
ourselves; all the gentlemen o'th' country shall be beholding
to us and our pastimes.   55

FALCONER

And we'll make your worship admire, sir.

39 *perfumer* one who fumigates or perfumes rooms
44 *Sa ho* a hawking cry
46 *There, boy* a hunting cry
49 *countenance* favour
53 *champion* champaign
56 *your* ed. you Q1
56 *admire* wonder

HOARD

Say'st thou so? do but make me admire, and thou shalt want
for nothing.—My tailor!

TAILOR

Anon, sir.

HOARD

Go presently in hand with the liveries.   60

TAILOR

I will, sir.

HOARD

My barber.

BARBER

Here, sir.

HOARD

Make 'em all trim fellows, louse 'em well—especially my
huntsman—and cut all their beards of the Polonian fashion.   65
—My perfumer.

PERFUMER

Under your nose, sir.

HOARD

Cast a better savour upon the knaves, to take away the scent
of my tailor's feet, and my barber's lotium-water.

PERFUMER

It shall be carefully performed, sir.   70

HOARD

But you, my falconer and huntsman, the welcom'st men
alive, i'faith!

HUNTSMAN

And we'll show you that, sir, shall deserve your worship's
favour.

HOARD

I prithee, show me that. Go, you knaves all, and wash your   75
lungs i'th' buttery, go. [*Exeunt* TAILOR, BARBER, PERFUMER,
FALCONER, *and* HUNTSMAN] By th' mass, and well remem-
bered, I'll ask my wife that question. Wife, Mistress Jane
Hoard!

Enter COURTESAN, *altered in apparel*

---

69 *lotium-water* stale urine, used as a hair-wash

---

65 *Polonian fashion.* Sampson quotes Fynes Moryson's *Itinerary*, 1617:
'The Polonians [Poles] shave all their heads close, excepting the haire
of the forehead, which they nourish very long and cast back to the hinder
part of the head.' Hoard is probably punning on 'pole', the traditional
symbol of the barber's profession.

COURTESAN

    Sir, would you with me?   80

HOARD

    I would but know, sweet wife, which might stand best to thy
    liking, to have the wedding dinner kept here or i'th' country?

COURTESAN

    Hum!—faith, sir, 'twould like me better here; here you were
    married, here let all rites be ended.

HOARD

    Could a marquess give a better answer? Hoard, bear thy head   85
    aloft, thou'st a wife will advance it.

                 [*Enter* HOST *with a letter*]

    What haste comes here now? Yea, a letter? Some dreg of my
    adversary's malice. Come hither; what's the news?

HOST

    A thing that concerns my mistress, sir. [*Gives letter to*
    COURTESAN]

HOARD

    Why then it concerns me, knave!   90

HOST

    Ay, and you, knave, too (cry your worship mercy): you are
    both like to come into trouble, I promise you, sir: a pre-
    contract.

HOARD

    How? a precontract, say'st thou?

HOST

    I fear they have too much proof on't, sir. Old Lucre, he runs   95
    mad up and down, and will to law as fast as he can; young
    Witgood laid hold on by his creditors, he exclaims upon you
    a't'other side, says you have wrought his undoing by the
    injurious detaining of his contract.

HOARD

    Body a' me!   100

HOST

    He will have utmost satisfaction;
    The law shall give him recompense, he says.

COURTESAN

    [*Aside*] Alas, his creditors so merciless! my state being yet
    uncertain, I deem it not unconscionable to furder him.

85 *marquess* marchioness
85–6 *bear . . . it* 'An unconscious allusion to the horns of the cuckold'
    (Spencer)   87 *Yea* ed. yee Qq
92 *precontract* legally binding betrothal agreement

HOST
  True, sir,—   105
HOARD
  Wife, what says that letter? Let me construe it.
COURTESAN
  Curst be my rash and unadvised words! [*Tears letter and
  stamps on it*]
  I'll set my foot upon my tongue,
  And tread my inconsiderate grant to dust.
HOARD
  Wife—   110
HOST
  [*Aside*] A pretty shift, i'faith! I commend a woman when
  she can make away a letter from her husband handsomely,
  and this was cleanly done, by my troth.
COURTESAN
  I did, sir!
  Some foolish words I must confess did pass,   115
  Which now litigiously he fastens on me.
HOARD
  Of what force? Let me examine 'em.
COURTESAN
  Too strong, I fear: would I were well freed of him!
HOARD
  Shall I compound?
COURTESAN
  No, sir, I'd have it done some nobler way   120
  Of your side; I'd have you come off with honour;
  Let baseness keep with them. Why, have you not
  The means, sir? The occasion's offered you.
HOARD
  Where? How, dear wife?
COURTESAN
  He is now caught by his creditors; the slave's needy, his   125
  debts petty; he'll rather bind himself to all inconveniences
  than rot in prison; by this only means you may get a release
  from him. 'Tis not yet come to his uncle's hearing; send
  speedily for the creditors; by this time he's desperate, he'll
  set his hand to anything: take order for his debts, or dis-   130
  charge 'em quite: a pax on him, let's be rid of a rascal!

113 *cleanly* adroitly
119 *compound* make a financial concession (in light of what follows, a
     long-standing arrangement is meant)
122-3 ed. prose in Qq

HOARD
    Excellent!
    Thou dost astonish me.—Go, run, make haste;
    Bring both the creditors and Witgood hither.
HOST
    [*Aside*] This will be some revenge yet.   [*Exit*] 135
HOARD
    In the mean space I'll have a release drawn.—Within there!

                    [*Enter* SERVANT]
SERVANT
    Sir?
HOARD
    Sirrah, come take directions; go to my scrivener.
COURTESAN
    [*Aside*] I'm yet like those whose riches lie in dreams;
    If I be waked, they're false; such is my fate,   140
    Who ventures deeper than the desperate state.
    Though I have sinned, yet could I become new,
    For, where I once vow, I am ever true.
HOARD
    Away, dispatch; on my displeasure, quickly. [*Exit* SERVANT]
    Happy occasion! Pray heaven he be in the right vein now to 145
    set his hand to't, that nothing alter him; grant that all his
    follies may meet in him at once, to besot him enough! I
    pray for him i'faith, and here he comes.

                [*Enter* WITGOOD *and* CREDITORS]
WITGOOD
    What would you with me now, my uncle's spiteful adversary?
HOARD
    Nay, I am friends.
WITGOOD   Ay, when your mischief's spent.   150
HOARD
    I heard you were arrested.

132–4 ed. prose in Qq
137 SERVANT ed. l. Qq
147–8 lineation ed. I . . . comes Qq as separate line
151–2 lineation ed.

138 *scrivener.* Not merely a penman, but a notary, and one who, like the
    lawyer and the usurer, lives on the misfortunes of others. 'An usurer is
    one that puts his money to the unnatural act of generation, and the
    scrivener is his bawd' (Tilley, U28). This general characterisation
    persisted—cf. Pope's *Epistle to Cobham*, l. 106: 'Will sneaks a Scriv'ner,
    an exceeding knave'.

WITGOOD   Well, what then?
  You will pay none of my debts, I am sure.
HOARD
  A wise man cannot tell;
  There may be those conditions 'greed upon
  May move me to do much.
WITGOOD   Ay, when?—   155
  'Tis thou, perjured woman! (Oh, no name
  Is vild enough to match thy treachery!)
  That art the cause of my confusion.
COURTESAN
  Out, you penurious slave!
HOARD
  Nay, wife, you are too froward;   160
  Let him alone; give losers leave to talk.
WITGOOD
  Shall I remember thee of another promise
  Far stronger than the first?
COURTESAN   I'd fain know that.
WITGOOD
  'Twould call shame to thy cheeks.
COURTESAN   Shame!
WITGOOD   Hark in your ear.
  —[*Draws* COURTESAN *aside*] Will he come off, think'st thou,   165
  and pay my debts roundly?
COURTESAN
  Doubt nothing; there's a release a-drawing and all, to which
  you must set your hand.
WITGOOD
  Excellent!
COURTESAN
  But methinks, i'faith, you might have made some shift to dis-   170
  charge this yourself, having in the mortgage, and never have
  burdened my conscience with it.
WITGOOD
  A' my troth, I could not, for my creditors' cruelties extend
  to the present.
COURTESAN
  No more.—   175
  Why, do your worst for that, I defy you.

155–6 lineation ed.
155 *when* exclamation of impatience   157 *vild* vile
161 *give . . . talk* proverbial   162–3 ed. prose in Qq
164–6 lineation ed.   175–6 lineation ed.

WITGOOD

Y'are impudent: I'll call up witnesses.

COURTESAN

Call up thy wits, for thou hast been devoted
To follies a long time.

HOARD   Wife, y'are too bitter.—

Master Witgood, and you, my masters, you shall hear a mild   180
speech come from me now, and this it is: 't 'as been my
fortune, gentlemen, to have an extraordinary blessing
poured upon me a'late, and here she stands; I have wedded
her and bedded her, and yet she is little the worse. Some
foolish words she hath passed to you in the country, and   185
some peevish debts you owe here in the city; set the hare's
head to the goose-giblet: release you her of her words, and
I'll release you of your debts, sir.

WITGOOD

Would you so? I thank you for that, sir; I cannot blame you,
i'faith.   190

HOARD

Why, are not debts better than words, sir?

WITGOOD

Are not words promises, and are not promises debts, sir?

HOARD

He plays at back-racket with me.

1 CREDITOR

Come hither, Master Witgood, come hither; be ruled by fools
once.   [CREDITORS *draw* WITGOOD *aside*]   195

2 CREDITOR

We are citizens, and know what belong to't.

1 CREDITOR

Take hold of his offer; pax on her, let her go. If your debts
were once discharged, I would help you to a widow myself
worth ten of her.

3 CREDITOR

Mass, partner, and now you remember me on't, there's   200
Master Mulligrub's sister newly fallen a widow.

178–9 ed. prose in Qq   186 *peevish* silly
186–7 *set . . . giblet* give tit for tat (proverbial)
193 *back-racket* the return of the ball in tennis, hence fig. a counter-
        charge, a *tu quoque*

---

201 *Mulligrub's.* Another example of Middleton's penchant for grotesque
    names. The mulligrubs was 'a fit of megrims or spleen' (*OED*). There
    is a Master Mulligrub in Marston's *The Dutch Courtesan*, 1605.

1 CREDITOR
Cuds me, as pat as can be! There's a widow left for you, ten
thousand in money, beside plate, jewels, *et cetera*; I warrant
it a match; we can do all in all with her. Prithee dispatch;
we'll carry thee to her presently.   205

WITGOOD
My uncle will never endure me, when he shall hear I set my
hand to a release.

2 CREDITOR
Hark, I'll tell thee a trick for that. I have spent five hundred
pound in suits in my time; I should be wise. Thou'rt now a
prisoner; make a release; take't of my word, whatsoever a   210
man makes as long as he is in durance, 'tis nothing in law,
not thus much.   [*Snaps his fingers*]

WITGOOD
Say you so, sir?

3 CREDITOR
I have paid for't, I know't.

WITGOOD
Proceed then, I consent.   215

3 CREDITOR
Why, well said.

HOARD
How now, my masters; what, have you done with him?

1 CREDITOR
With much ado, sir, we have got him to consent.

HOARD
Ah-a-a! and what came his debts to now?

1 CREDITOR
Some eight score odd pounds, sir.   220

HOARD
Naw, naw, naw, naw, naw! Tell me the second time; give me
a lighter sum. They are but desperate debts, you know,
never called in but upon such an accident; a poor, needy
knave, he would starve and rot in prison. Come, come, you
shall have ten shillings in the pound, and the sum down   225
roundly.

1 CREDITOR
You must make it a mark, sir.

HOARD
Go to, then; tell your money in the mean time; you shall find

202 *Cuds* see II. i, 40
222 *desperate* 'bad', i.e. irretrievable
227 *mark* see III. i, 130

little less there.—Come, Master Witgood, you are so
unwilling to do yourself good now.   230

[*Enter* SCRIVENER]

Welcome, honest scrivener.—Now you shall hear the release
read.

SCRIVENER

[*Reads*] Be it known to all men by these presents, that I,
Theodorus Witgood, gentleman, sole nephew to Pecunius
Lucre, having unjustly made title and claim to one Jane   235
Medler, late widow of Anthony Medler, and now wife to
Walkadine Hoard, in consideration of a competent sum of
money to discharge my debts, do forever hereafter disclaim
any title, right, estate, or interest in or to the said widow,
late in the occupation of the said Anthony Medler, and now   240
in the occupation of Walkadine Hoard; as also neither to lay
claim by virtue of any former contract, grant, promise, or
demise, to any of her manors, manor houses, parks, groves,
meadow-grounds, arable lands, barns, stacks, stables, dove-
holes, and coney-burrows; together with all her cattle,   245
money, plate, jewels, borders, chains, bracelets, furnitures,
hangings, moveables, or immoveables. In witness whereof I,
the said Theodorus Witgood, have interchangeably set to
my hand and seal before these presents, the day and date
above written.   250

WITGOOD

What a precious fortune hast thou slipped here, like a beast
as thou art!

HOARD

Come, unwilling heart, come.

WITGOOD

Well, Master Hoard, give me the pen; I see
'Tis vain to quarrel with our destiny. [*Signs*]   255

HOARD

Oh, as vain a thing as can be; you cannot commit a greater
absurdity, sir. So, so; give me that hand now: before all
these presents, I am friends forever with thee.

233 *presents* the present document (*OED*, 'present', *sb.*¹ 2. b.)
243 *demise* conveyance or transfer of an estate by will or lease
243 *manors* ed. Mannor Qq   244 *dove-holes* dove-houses
245 *coney-burrows* rabbit warrens
245 *cattle* chattels (*OED*, 'cattle', *sb.*, 3)
247 *immoveables* ed. immouerables Q1
249 *presents* witnesses (*OED* 'present', *sb.*¹, 2)
251 *slipped* let slip

WITGOOD
Troth, and it were pity of my heart now, if I should bear you
any grudge, i'faith.   260

HOARD
Content. I'll send for thy uncle against the wedding dinner;
we will be friends once again.

WITGOOD
I hope to bring it to pass myself, sir.

HOARD
How now? is't right, my masters?

1 CREDITOR
'Tis something wanting, sir; yet it shall be sufficient.   265

HOARD
Why, well said; a good conscience makes a fine show
nowadays. Come, my masters, you shall all taste of my wine
ere you depart.

ALL
We follow you, sir.
                    [Exeunt HOARD, COURTESAN and SCRIVENER]

WITGOOD
[Aside] I'll try these fellows now.—A word, sir; what, will   270
you carry me to that rich widow now?

1 CREDITOR
Why, do you think we were in earnest, i'faith? Carry you to a
rich widow? We should get much credit by that: a noted
rioter! a contemptible prodigal! 'Twas a trick we have
amongst us to get in our money. Fare you well, sir.   275
                                        Exeunt [CREDITORS]

WITGOOD
Farewell, and be hanged, you short pig-haired, ram-headed
rascals! He that believes in you shall never be saved, I warrant
him. By this new league I shall have some access unto my love.
                            She is above

NIECE
Master Witgood!

WITGOOD
My life!   280

NIECE
Meet me presently; that note directs you [throwing it down];
I would not be suspected. Our happiness attends us. Farewell!

WITGOOD
A word's enough.   Exeunt

276 pig-haired the citizens wore their hair short
276 ram-headed cuckolded   283 s.d. after l. 282 in Qq

[Act IV, Scene v]

DAMPIT, *the usurer, in his bed;* AUDREY *spinning by;* [BOY]
Song [*by* AUDREY]

Let the usurer cram him, in interest that excel,
There's pits enow to damn him, before he comes to hell;
In Holborn some, in Fleet Street some,
Where'er he come, there's some, there's some.

DAMPIT

Trahe, traheto, draw the curtain, give me a sip of sack more.   5

Enter GENTLEMEN [*i.e.,* LAMPREY *and* SPITCHCOCK]

LAMPREY

Look you, did not I tell you he lay like the devil in chains,
when he was bound for a thousand year?

SPITCHCOCK

But I think the devil had no steel bedstaffs; he goes beyond
him for that.

LAMPREY

Nay, do but mark the conceit of his drinking; one must wipe   10
his mouth for him with a muckinder, do you see, sir?

2 *pits* brothels and taverns
3 *Holborn . . . Fleet Street* where Dampit conducted his business.
Cf. I. iv, 57–8
8 *bedstaffs* stout staves laid loose across the old wooden bedsteads,
to support the bedding
10 *conceit* peculiarity   11 *muckinder* handkerchief or bib

---

s.d. He would have been 'discovered' on the inner stage when the curtain
he refers to was drawn back.
1–4 The song is by Thomas Ravenscroft, a chorister at Paul's, and is
reprinted in 'Melismata' (1611), a collection of his lyrics. In Q1, it lacks
the first two lines, probably as a result of a compositor's blunder. They
run:
My master is so wise, so wise, that he's proceeded wittol,
My mistress is a fool, a fool, and yet 'tis the most get-all.
See A. J. Sabol, 'Ravenscroft's "Melismata" and the Children of
Paul's', *RN*, XII (1959), 3–9.
6–7 See *Revelation*, xx, 2. Sampson suggests that Dampit is chained to the
'great iron chest' (III. iv, 5), but it is unlikely that the Biblical reference
need be taken so literally, especially in the light of the s.d. which opens
this scene. Further, 'hanging in chains' seems to have been a traditional
end for the usurer: see Dekker's *Work for Armourers* (*The Non-Dramatic
Works*, ed. Grosart, iv, 164) and his *If This Be Not a Good Play, the
Devil Is In It*, V. iv, 253–4.

SPITCHCOCK
Is this the sick trampler? Why, he is only bed-rid with
drinking.

LAMPREY
True, sir. He spies us.

DAMPIT
What, sir Tristram? You come and see a weak man here, a   15
very weak man.

LAMPREY
If you be weak in body, you should be strong in prayer, sir.

DAMPIT
Oh, I have prayed too much, poor man.

LAMPREY
There's a taste of his soul for you.

SPITCHCOCK
Fah, loathsome!   20

LAMPREY
I come to borrow a hundred pound of you, sir.

DAMPIT
Alas, you come at an ill time; I cannot spare it, i'faith; I ha'
but two thousand i'th' house.

AUDREY
Ha, ha, ha!

DAMPIT
Out, you gernative quean, the mullipood of villainy, the   25
spinner of concupiscency!

Enter other GENTLEMAN [*i.e.,* SIR LANCELOT]

LANCELOT
Yea, gentlemen, are you here before us? How is he now?

LAMPREY
Faith, the same man still: the tavern bitch has bit him i'th'
head.

12 *trampler* See I. iv, 10
25 *gernative* addicted to 'girning', or grumbling
25 *mullipood* dirty toad (?). See *OED, s.v. mull* and *pode*
27 *Yea* ed. Yee Qq   28–9 *tavern . . . head* he is drunk (proverbial)

---

15 *Tristram.* In the various revivals of the Tristram story which began in
the late 15th century, the famous lover had become a mere gallant, and
his name was loosely applied to any libertine. Lamprey does not display
a licentious bent in the play: Dampit is simply playing on his name,
lampreys supposedly being strongly aphrodisiac.
26 *spinner.* Audrey is literally spinning, but *spinner* probably = *spider*
here. See I. i, 31.

LANCELOT

We shall have the better sport with him; peace!—And how   30
cheers Master Dampit now?

DAMPIT

Oh, my bosom Sir Lancelot, how cheer I! Thy presence is
restorative.

LANCELOT

But I hear a great complaint of you, Master Dampit, among
gallants.   35

DAMPIT

I am glad of that, i'faith; prithee, what?

LANCELOT

They say you are waxed proud a' late, and if a friend visit you
in the afternoon, you'll scarce know him.

DAMPIT

Fie, fie! Proud? I cannot remember any such thing; sure I
was drunk then.   40

LANCELOT

Think you so, sir?

DAMPIT

There 'twas, i'faith, nothing but the pride of the sack, and so
certify 'em.—Fetch sack, sirrah!

BOY

A vengeance sack you once!

                    [*Exit, and returns presently with sack*]

AUDREY

Why, Master Dampit, if you hold on as you begin, and lie a   45
little longer, you need not take care how to dispose your
wealth; you'll make the vintner your heir.

DAMPIT

Out, you babliaminy, you unfeathered, cremitoried quean,
you cullisance of scabiosity!

AUDREY

Good words, Master Dampit, to speak before a maid and a   50
virgin.

DAMPIT

Hang thy virginity upon the pole of carnality!

---

48 *babliaminy* babbler
48 *cremitoried* 'burnt, syphilitic. *Unfeathered* implies that she has lost
      her hair from the pox' (Spencer)
49 *cullisance* a corruption of *cognizance* = heraldic badge
49 *scabiosity* syphilis

AUDREY
   Sweet terms! My mistress shall know 'em.

LAMPREY
   Note but the misery of this usuring slave: here he lies, like a
   noisome dunghill, full of the poison of his drunken blas-   55
   phemies, and they to whom he bequeaths all grudge him the
   very meat that feeds him, the very pillow that eases him.
   Here may a usurer behold his end. What profits it to be a
   slave in this world, and a devil i'th' next?

DAMPIT
   Sir Lancelot, let me buss thee, Sir Lancelot; thou art the only   60
   friend that I honour and respect.

LANCELOT
   I thank you for that, Master Dampit.

DAMPIT
   Farewell, my bosom Sir Lancelot.

LANCELOT
   Gentlemen, an you love me, let me step behind you, and one
   of you fall a-talking of me to him.   65

LAMPREY
   Content.—Master Dampit.

DAMPIT
   So, sir.

LAMPREY
   Here came Sir Lancelot to see you e'en now.

DAMPIT
   Hang him, rascal!

LAMPREY
   Who, Sir Lancelot?   70

DAMPIT
   Pythagorical rascal!

LAMPREY
   Pythagorical?

DAMPIT
   Ay, he changes his cloak when he meets a sergeant.

---

60 *buss* kiss

53 *My mistress*. This is the only time that we hear of Dampit's wife. It may
   be an authorial slip, an example of episodic intensification. But see note
   on IV. v, 1–4 above.
71–3 A debasement of the Pythagorean doctrine of the transmigration of
   souls. Cf. Jonson's *Cynthia's Revels*, 1601, IV. iii, 146; and Middleton's
   Your Five Gallants, 1605, V. i, 108–9: 'That Pythagorical rascal! in a
   gentleman's suit today, in a knight's tomorrow.'

LANCELOT
   What a rogue's this!
LAMPREY
   I wonder you can rail at him, sir; he comes in love to see you.   75
DAMPIT
   A louse for his love! His father was a comb-maker; I have no
   need of his crawling love. He comes to have longer day, the
   superlative rascal!
LANCELOT
   'Sfoot, I can no longer endure the rogue!—Master Dampit,
   I come to take my leave once again, sir.   80
DAMPIT
   Who? my dear and kind Sir Lancelot, the only gentleman of
   England? Let me hug thee; farewell, and a thousand.
LAMPREY
   Composed of wrongs and slavish flatteries!
LANCELOT
   Nay, gentlemen, he shall show you more tricks yet; I'll give
   you another taste of him.   85
LAMPREY
   Is't possible?
LANCELOT
   His memory is upon departing.
DAMPIT
   Another cup of sack!
LANCELOT
   Mass, then 'twill be quite gone! Before he drink that, tell him
   there's a country client come up, and here attends for his   90
   learned advice.
LAMPREY
   Enough.
DAMPIT
   One cup more, and then let the bell toll; I hope I shall be
   weak enough by that time.
LAMPREY
   Master Dampit.   95
DAMPIT
   Is the sack spouting?
LAMPREY
   'Tis coming forward, sir. Here's a countryman, a client of
   yours, waits for your deep and profound advice, sir.

77 *crawling* continuing the *louse* image
77 *longer day* more time to pay off his debts
82 *farewell . . . thousand* a thousand times farewell

DAMPIT
A coxcombry? Where is he? Let him approach; set me up a
peg higher.   100

LAMPREY
You must draw near, sir.

DAMPIT
Now, good man fooliaminy, what say you to me now?

LANCELOT
Please your good worship, I am a poor man, sir—

DAMPIT
What make you in my chamber then?

LANCELOT
I would entreat your worship's device in a just and honest   105
cause, sir.

DAMPIT
I meddle with no such matters; I refer 'em to Master No-
man's office.

LANCELOT
I had but one house left me in all the world, sir, which was
my father's, my grandfather's, my great-grandfather's; and   110
now a villain has unjustly wrung me out, and took possession
on't.

DAMPIT
Has he such feats? Thy best course is to bring thy *ejectione
firmae*, and in seven year thou may'st shove him out by the
law.   115

LANCELOT
Alas, an't please your worship, I have small friends and less
money.

DAMPIT
Hoyday! this gear will fadge well. Hast no money? Why,
then, my advice is thou must set fire o'th' house and so get
him out.   120

LAMPREY
That will break strife, indeed.

104 *make* do
105 *device* an intentional malapropism
113–14 *ejectione firmae* writ of ejectment whereby a person ousted
     from an estate for years may recover possession of it
114 *firmae* ed. *firme* Qq
118 *gear* business
118 *fadge* succeed
121 *break* broach, breech

LANCELOT

I thank your worship for your hot counsel, sir.—Altering but
my voice a little, you see he knew me not; you may observe
by this that a drunkard's memory holds longer in the voice
than in the person. But, gentlemen, shall I show you a sight?   125
Behold the little dive-dapper of damnation, Gulf the
usurer, for his time worse than t'other.

Enter HOARD *with* GULF

LAMPREY

What's he comes with him?

LANCELOT

Why, Hoard, that married lately the Widow Medler.

LAMPREY

Oh, I cry you mercy, sir.   130

HOARD

Now, gentlemen visitants, how does Master Dampit?

LANCELOT

Faith, here he lies e'en drawing in, sir, good canary as fast as
he can, sir; a very weak creature, truly, he is almost past
memory.

HOARD

Fie, Master Dampit! you lie lazing abed here, and I come to   135
invite you to my wedding dinner; up, up, up!

DAMPIT

Who's this? Master Hoard? Who hast thou married, in the
name of foolery?

HOARD

A rich widow.

DAMPIT

A Dutch widow?   140

HOARD

A rich widow; one Widow Medler.

DAMPIT

Medler? She keeps open house.

HOARD

She did, I can tell you, in her tother husband's days; open
house for all comers; horse and man was welcome, and room
enough for 'em all.   145

126 *dive-dapper* dabchick, a small diving waterfowl
127 *for his time* considering the duration of his activities
132 *canary* a light, sweet wine from the Canary Islands
142 *open house* see II. ii, 59

DAMPIT

There's too much for thee, then; thou may'st let out some to
thy neighbours.

GULF

What, hung alive in chains? O spectacle! bed-staffs of steel?
O monstrum horrendum, informe, ingens, cui lumen ademptum!
O Dampit, Dampit, here's a just judgement shown upon   150
usury, extortion, and trampling villainy!

LANCELOT

This is excellent, thief rails upon the thief!

GULF

Is this the end of cut-throat usury, brothel, and blasphemy?
Now may'st thou see what race a usurer runs.

DAMPIT

Why, thou rogue of universality, do not I know thee? Thy   155
sound is like the cuckoo, the Welsh ambassador; thou
cowardly slave, that offers to fight with a sick man when his
weapon's down! Rail upon me in my naked bed? Why, thou
great Lucifer's little vicar, I am not so weak but I know a
knave at first sight. Thou inconscionable rascal! thou that 160
goest upon Middlesex juries, and will make haste to give up
thy verdict, because thou wilt not lose thy dinner, are you
answered?

GULF

An't were not for shame—   *draws his dagger*

---

149 *O . . . ademptum* O fearful monster, misshapen, huge, deprived of
      sight (*Aeneid*, III. 658)
152 *This is excellent* ed. This exlent Qq
153–4 lineation ed. Is . . . Vsury Qq as separate line
158 *upon . . . bed* upon me undressed in bed

---

156 *cuckoo . . . ambassador.* Welsh raiding bands used to descend on the
      English border to fight and plunder 'about Cuckoe tymes', according to
      an anonymous play *The Welsh Ambassador*, 1623. See Gwyn Williams,
      'The Cuckoo, the Welsh Ambassador', *MLR*, LI (1956), 223–5.
158 *naked bed.* An allusion to Hieronimo's much-ridiculed line in Kyd's
      The Spanish Tragedy, 1587, II. v, i: 'What outcries pluck me from my
      naked bed . . . ?'
161 *Middlesex juries.* Frequently a subject for complaints. Cf. Ben Jonson's
      Every Man in His Humour, 1616, I. ii, 88–9, and Herford and Simpson's
      note (ix, 350), in which they quote the reputed saying of a Tudor bishop:
      'A London jury would find Abel guilty of the murder of Cain'. And see
      Tilley, J104: 'A London (Kentish, Middlesex) jury hang half and save
      alf.'

DAMPIT
   Thou wouldst be hanged then.   165
LAMPREY
   Nay, you must exercise patience, Master Gulf, always, in a
   sick man's chamber.
LANCELOT
   He'll quarrel with none, I warrant you, but those that are
   bed-rid.
DAMPIT
   Let him come, gentlemen, I am armed; reach my close-stool   170
   hither.
LANCELOT
   Here will be a sweet fray anon; I'll leave you, gentlemen.
LAMPREY
   Nay, we'll along with you.—Master Gulf—
GULF
   Hang him, usuring rascal!
LANCELOT
   Push, set your strength to his, your wit to his.   175
AUDREY
   Pray, gentlemen, depart; his hour's come upon him.—Sleep
   in my bosom, sleep.
LANCELOT
   Nay, we have enough of him, i'faith; keep him for the house.
   Now make your best.
   For thrice his wealth I would not have his breast.   180
GULF
   A little thing would make me beat him, now he's asleep.
LANCELOT
   Mass, then 'twill be a pitiful day when he wakes. I would be
   loath to see that day come.
GULF
   You overrule me, gentlemen, i'faith.   *Exeunt*

[Act V, Scene i]

Enter LUCRE *and* WITGOOD

WITGOOD
   Nay, uncle, let me prevail with you so much;
   I'faith, go, now he has invited you.

172 *sweet* with reference to its odoriferous possibilities
176 *his . . . him* he is on the point of death
184 GULF ed. L*u*l: Q1   s.d. ed. *ACTVS.* Qq

LUCRE
I shall have great joy there when he has borne away the
widow.
WITGOOD
Why, la, I thought where I should find you presently; uncle,   5
a' my troth, 'tis nothing so.
LUCRE
What's nothing so, sir? Is not he married to the widow?
WITGOOD
No, by my troth, is he not, uncle.
LUCRE
How?
WITGOOD
Will you have the truth on't? He is married to a whore,   10
i'faith.
LUCRE
I should laugh at that.
WITGOOD
Uncle, let me perish in your favour if you find it not so, and
that 'tis I that have married the honest woman.
LUCRE
Ha! I'd walk ten mile a' foot to see that, i'faith.   15
WITGOOD
And see't you shall, or I'll never see you again.
LUCRE
A quean, i'faith? Ha, ha, ha!   *Exeunt*

[Act V, Scene ii]

Enter HOARD, *tasting wine, the* HOST *following in a livery cloak*

HOARD
Pup, pup, pup, pup! I like not this wine. Is there never a
better tierce in the house?
HOST
Yes, sir, there are as good tierce in the house as any are in
England.
HOARD
Desire your mistress, you knave, to taste 'em all over; she has   5
better skill.

2 *tierce* cask. The host puns in the following lines on other meanings
   of the word: a band or company (of soldiers), or a thrust in
   fencing

HOST

    [*Aside*] Has she so? The better for her, and the worse for you.

                                       Exit

HOARD

    Arthur!

               [*Enter* ARTHUR]

    Is the cupboard of plate set out?

ARTHUR

    All's in order, sir.   [*Exit*]   10

HOARD

    I am in love with my liveries every time I think on 'em; they
make a gallant show, by my troth.—Niece!

              [*Enter* NIECE]

NIECE

    Do you call, sir?

HOARD

    Prithee, show a little diligence, and overlook the knaves a
little; they'll filch and steal today, and send whole pasties   15
home to their wives; an thou beest a good niece, do not see
me purloined.

NIECE

    Fear it not, sir.—[*Aside*] I have cause: though the feast be
prepared for you, yet it serves fit for my wedding dinner too.

                                     [*Exit*]

    Enter two Gentlemen [*i.e.*, LAMPREY *and* SPITCHCOCK]

HOARD

    Master Lamprey and Master Spitchcock, two the most   20
welcome gentlemen alive! Your fathers and mine were all
free o'th'fishmongers.

LAMPREY

    They were indeed, sir. You see bold guests, sir, soon
entreated.

HOARD

    And that's best, sir.—   25

              [*Enter* SERVANT]

    How now, sirrah?

  9 *cupboard of plate* a side-board for the display of plate, or the
     service of plate itself
  22 *free o'th' fishmongers* members of that one of the great city com-
     panies (with an obvious allusion to the 'fishiness' of the names—
     see I. iii, first s.d. and note)

SERVANT
There's a coach come to th'door, sir.   [*Exit*]

HOARD
My Lady Foxstone, a' my life!—Mistress Jane Hoard, wife!
—Mass, 'tis her Ladyship indeed!

[*Enter* LADY FOXSTONE]

Madam, you are welcome to an unfurnished house, dearth of   30
cheer, scarcity of attendance.

LADY FOXSTONE
You are pleased to make the worst, sir.

HOARD
Wife!

[*Enter* COURTESAN]

LADY FOXSTONE
Is this your bride?

HOARD
Yes, madam.—Salute my Lady Foxstone.   35

COURTESAN
Please you, madam, a while to taste the air in the garden?

LADY FOXSTONE
'Twill please us well. *Exeunt* [LADY FOXSTONE *and* COURTESAN]

HOARD
Who would not wed? The most delicious life!
No joys are like the comforts of a wife.

LAMPREY
So we bachelors think, that are not troubled with them.   40

[*Enter* SERVANT]

SERVANT
Your worship's brother with another ancient gentleman are
newly alighted, sir.   [*Exit*]

HOARD
Master Onesiphorus Hoard? Why, now our company begins
to come in.

[*Enter* ONESIPHORUS HOARD, LIMBER *and* KIX]

My dear and kind brother, welcome, i'faith.   45

35 *Foxstone* ed. *Foxtone* Qq

41 *another ancient gentleman.* The servant may have only noticed one old
man with Onesiphorus, but all the evidence is that Middleton was
careless about the introduction and numbering of his minor characters.
See III. iii, first s.d.

ONESIPHORUS
You see we are men at an hour, brother.

HOARD
Ay, I'll say that for you, brother; you keep as good an hour
to come to a feast as any gentleman in the shire.—What, old
Master Limber and Master Kix! Do we meet, i'faith, jolly
gentlemen?   50

LIMBER
We hope you lack guests, sir?

HOARD
Oh, welcome, welcome! we lack still such guests as your
worships.

ONESIPHORUS
Ah, sirrah brother, have you catched up Widow Medler?

HOARD
From 'em all, brother; and I may tell you, I had mighty   55
enemies, those that stuck sore; old Lucre is a sore fox, I can
tell you, brother.

ONESIPHORUS
Where is she? I'll go seek her out; I long to have a smack at
her lips.

HOARD
And most wishfully, brother, see where she comes.   60

[*Enter* COURTESAN *and* LADY FOXSTONE]

Give her a smack now we may hear it all the house over.

Both [i.e., COURTESAN *and* ONESIPHORUS HOARD] *turn back*

COURTESAN
Oh, heaven, I am betrayed! I know that face.

HOARD
Ha, ha, ha! Why, how now? Are you both ashamed?—Come,
gentlemen, we'll look another way.

ONESIPHORUS
Nay, brother, hark you: come, y'are disposed to be merry?   65

HOARD
Why do we meet else, man?

ONESIPHORUS
That's another matter; I was never so 'fraid in my life but
that you had been in earnest.

HOARD
How mean you, brother?

61 *smack* ed. smerck Qq

ONESIPHORUS
   You said she was your wife?   70

HOARD
   Did I so? By my troth, and so she is.

ONESIPHORUS
   By your troth, brother?

HOARD
   What reason have I to dissemble with my friends, brother?
   If marriage can make her mine, she is mine! Why?

ONESIPHORUS
   Troth, I am not well of a sudden. I must crave pardon,   75
   brother; I came to see you but I cannot stay dinner, i'faith.

HOARD
   I hope you will not serve me so, brother.

LIMBER
   By your leave, Master Hoard—

HOARD
   What now? what now? Pray, gentlemen, you were wont to
   show yourselves wise men.   80

LIMBER
   But you have shown your folly too much here.

HOARD
   How?

KIX
   Fie, fie! A man of your repute and name!
   You'll feast your friends, but cloy 'em first with shame.

HOARD
   This grows too deep; pray, let us reach the sense.   85

LIMBER
   In your old age dote on a courtesan—

HOARD
   Ha?

KIX
   Marry a strumpet!

HOARD
   Gentlemen!

ONESIPHORUS
   And Witgood's quean!   90

HOARD
   Oh! nor lands, nor living?

ONESIPHORUS
   Living!

HOARD
   [to COURTESAN] Speak!

COURTESAN
Alas, you know at first, sir,
I told you I had nothing.   95
HOARD
Out, out! I am cheated; infinitely cozened!
LIMBER
Nay, Master Hoard—

Enter WITGOOD *and* LUCRE

HOARD
A Dutch widow, a Dutch widow, a Dutch widow!
LUCRE
Why, nephew, shall I trace thee still a liar?
Wilt make me mad? Is not yon thing the widow?   100
WITGOOD
Why, la, you are so hard a' belief, uncle!
By my troth, she's a whore.
LUCRE   Then thou'rt a knave.
WITGOOD
Negatur argumentum, uncle.
LUCRE
Probo tibi, nephew: he that knows a woman to be a quean
must needs be a knave; thou say'st thou know'st her to be   105
one; *ergo*, if she be a quean, thou'rt a knave.
WITGOOD
Negatur sequela majoris, uncle, he that knows a woman to be
a quean must needs be a knave; I deny that.
HOARD
Lucre and Witgood, y'are both villains; get you out of my
house!   110
LUCRE
Why, didst not invite me to thy wedding dinner?
WITGOOD
And are not you and I sworn perpetual friends before witness,
sir, and were both drunk upon't?
HOARD
Daintily abused! Y'ave put a junt upon me!

99–102 ed. prose in Qq
103 *Negatur argumentum* Proof is denied
104 *Probo tibi* I'll prove it to you (*Probo* . . . Nephew Qq as separate
line)
107 *Negatur sequela majoris* The conclusion of your major premise is
denied
114 *junt* trick

LUCRE
    Ha, ha, ha!
HOARD   A common strumpet!
WITGOOD   Nay, now   115
    You wrong her, sir; if I were she, I'd have
    The law on you for that; I durst depose for her
    She ne'er had common use, nor common thought.
COURTESAN
    Despise me, publish me: I am your wife;
    What shame can I have now but you'll have part?   120
    If in disgrace you share, I sought not you;
    You pursued me, nay, forced me;
    Had I friends would follow it,
    Less than your action has been proved a rape.
ONESIPHORUS
    Brother!   125
COURTESAN
    Nor did I ever boast of lands unto you,
    Money, or goods; I took a plainer course
    And told you true I'd nothing.
    If error were committed, 'twas by you;
    Thank your own folly. Nor has my sin been   130
    So odious but worse has been forgiven;
    Nor am I so deformed but I may challenge
    The utmost power of any old man's love.—
    She that tastes not sin before, twenty to one but she'll taste
    it after; most of you old men are content to marry young 135
    virgins, and take that which follows; where, marrying one
    of us, you both save a sinner, and are quit from a cuckold for
    ever.
    And more, in brief, let this your best thoughts win,
    She that knows sin, knows best how to hate sin.   140
HOARD
    Cursed be all malice! Black are the fruits of spite,

115–18 ed. prose in Qq
119 *publish* denounce, 'show up'
130–3 ed. prose in Qq
136 *where* whereas
137 *quit from* saved from the danger of becoming

139–40 Q1 has inverted commas before these lines to emphasise their
    sententious character. This was a fashionable practice in certain printing
    houses of the time; but the commas might well have been in Middleton's
    MS, if, as seems likely, he wanted to emphasise the artificiality of the
    speeches of 'repentance'.

And poison first their owners. Oh, my friends,
I must embrace shame, to be rid of shame!
Concealed disgrace prevents a public name.
Ah, Witgood! ah, Theodorus.   145

WITGOOD

Alas, sir, I was pricked in conscience to see her well
bestowed, and where could I bestow her better than upon
your pitiful worship? Excepting but myself, I dare swear
she's a virgin; and now, by marrying your niece, I have
banished myself for ever from her. She's mine aunt now, by   150
my faith, and there's no meddling with mine aunt, you know
—a sin against my nuncle.

COURTESAN

[*kneeling*] Lo, gentlemen, before you all
In true reclaiméd form I fall.
Henceforth for ever I defy   155
The glances of a sinful eye,
Waving of fans (which some suppose
Tricks of fancy), treading of toes,
Wringing of fingers, biting the lip
The wanton gait, th'alluring trip,   160
All secret friends and private meetings,
Close-borne letters and bawds' greetings,
Feigning excuse to women's labours
When we are sent for to th'next neighbours,
Taking false physic, and ne'er start   165

150 *aunt* pun on *aunt* = *mistress*
152 *nuncle* a common corruption of *uncle*
155 *defy* renounce
158 *fancy* love
159 *wringing* clasping
161 *friends* lovers
162 *Close* secretly

156–7 Cf. the Palinode to Jonson's *Cynthia's Revels:* 'From wauing of
fannes, coy glaunces, glickes, cringes, and all such simpring humours
. . . Good MERCVRY defend vs.'
158–9 Cf. Dekker's and Webster's *Northward Ho!*, II. ii, 11ff.: 'what
treads of the toe, salutations by winckes, discourse by bitings of the
lip, amorous glances, sweete stolne kisses when your husbands backs
turn'd, would passe betweene them.' See also III. ii, 109: 'Marke how
she wrings him by the fingers.'
163–4 Another frequently mentioned wifely deceit—see Nashe's *Christ's
Tears over Jerusalem*, 1593, (McKerrow, ii, 151), and Middleton's own
Black Book, 1604, (Bullen, viii, 35).

To be let blood, though sign be at heart,
Removing chambers, shifting beds,
To welcome friends in husbands' steads,
Them to enjoy, and you to marry,
They first served, while you must tarry,   170
They to spend, and you to gather,
They to get, and you to father—
These and thousand thousand more,
New reclaimed, I now abhor.

LUCRE
Ah, here's a lesson, rioter, for you.   175

WITGOOD
[kneeling] I must confess my follies; I'll down too.
And here for ever I disclaim
The cause of youth's undoing, game,
Chiefly dice, those true outlanders,
That shake out beggars, thieves, and panders,   180
Soul-wasting surfeits, sinful riots,
Queans' evils, doctors' diets,
'Pothecaries' drugs, surgeons' glisters,
Stabbing of arms for a common mistress,
Riband favours, ribald speeches,   185
Dear perfumed jackets, penniless breeches,
Dutch flapdragons, healths in urine,

179 *outlanders* foreigners
182 *Queans' evils* syphilis. 'A quibbling antithesis to king's evil'
   (Sampson). Cf. *Macbeth*, IV. iii, 146
186 *perfumed jackets* see IV. iii, 27
187 *flapdragons* raisins, or similar objects, set on fire and drunk in wine
   as they flamed. Dutchmen were supposed to be experts in the art
187 *healths . . . urine* another extravagance of the gallants; it was
   drunk mixed with wine

---

166 Hence dangerous. 'According to the directions for bleeding in old
   almanacs, blood was to be taken from particular parts under particular
   planets' (Dyce). Cf. *Northward Ho!*, III. i, 129–32: 'how many seuerall
   loues of Plaiers, of Vaulters, of Lieutenants haue I entertain'd . . . and
   now to let bloud when the signe is at the heart?'
183 *glisters*. Suppositories, enemas. Greene in *A Quip for an Upstart
   Courtier* sneers at the taking of clysters as being an affectation of the
   would be gallant (see Grosart, xi, 248).
184 *Stabbing of arms*. Drinking the blood mixed with wine in a health to
   one's mistress was a common practice. Cf. the palinode to *Cynthia's
   Revels:* 'From stabbing of armes, flap-dragons, healths, whiffes, and all
   such swaggering humours . . . Good MERCVRY defend vs', and Marston's
   The Dutch Courtesan, 1605, IV. i.

Drabs that keep a man too sure in—
I do defy you all.
Lend me each honest hand, for here I rise   190
A reclaimed man, loathing the general vice.

HOARD

So, so, all friends! The wedding dinner cools.
Who seem most crafty prove oft times most fools.   [*Exeunt*]

FINIS

Printed in Great Britain by
The Garden City Press Limited,
Letchworth, Hertfordshire